Praise for *Digging Deeper Into Action Research*

"This book supports teacher researchers in 'living the life of an inquirer' by providing specific advice for designing, conducting, and sharing the results of inquiries that are focused on student learning, as well as empowering practitioners to add their voices and knowledge to an educational field that is ready to push back against the misinformed, rigid, anti-teacher rhetoric that is currently all the rage in the U.S."

—Gail V. Ritchie, Instructional Coach
Fairfax County Public Schools, VA

"This book is an essential companion resource and provides the right supports for teachers as they investigate the world of teacher inquiry and action research. It also is capable of standing on its own for teachers who are just beginning their journeys into the world of action research. It is easy to read, provides a clear learning and teaching target and makes a compelling argument for teachers to investigate inquiry and data analysis in the classroom."

—Jana Scott Lindsay, Educational
Consultant-Curriculum and Instruction
Saskatoon Public Schools, Saskatchewan, Canada

"Nancy Dana has done it again! In clear, accessible, and empowering ways, Dana uses Digging Deeper Into Action Research to build on her substantial body of work in the field of practitioner research. Speaking to experienced teacher researchers, those new to the concept of teacher research, graduate students, undergraduates, school-based instructional coaches, and a host of others, Dana reiterates the essential components from her other books while allowing the reader a plethora of reflective, yet practical, exercises to deepen the work of practitioner inquiry. I cannot wait to share this book with my university and school-based colleagues, to use it with my students, and to re-engage with the process of teacher research myself!"

—Ryan Flessner, Assistant Professor of Teacher Education
College of Education, Butler University, Indianapolis, IN

"Dana's experience in inquiry, skills in research, focus on collaboration, and professional and respectful approach give it the power and authenticity needed to be effective. This professional and respectful approach accomplishes her goal for teacher inquirers to 'engage, enable, expand, express, and embrace.' The text engages learners of inquiry; the scaffolded approach enables inquirers to build their skills; the questions expand thinking; the examples, charts, and outlines provide guidance in practicing inquiry; and the depth of the text and references embrace the complexity of both teaching and inquiry. As educators, we look for ways not only to inform, but also to inspire. This teacher inquirers' field guide accomplishes both."

—Julie Rainer Dangel, Professor of Early Childhood Education
Georgia State University, Atlanta, GA

"Digging Deeper Into Action Research *will serve as a guide for teachers and inquiry coaches in our district as we strive to produce powerful, results-driven, inquiry-oriented professional learning communities as a professional growth process within our evaluation system."*

—Chris Borgen, Superintendent
Anacortes School District, Anacortes, WA

—Jennie Beltramini, Anacortes School District Teacher Association President and Washington Education Association Board Member
Anacortes, WA

"This text is an invaluable resource, equally appropriate for those engaged in inquiry and for those coaching others in the inquiry process. In the book and in the accompanying video features, readers will learn from the example of real teachers engaged in and learning from the research process. This is the resource we have been waiting for!"

—Cynthia Carver, Assistant Professor
Educational Leadership Department, Oakland University,
Rochester, MI

"Dana has created a smart, go-to field guide that offers busy practitioners an inspiring, yet practical, approach to thoughtful pursuit of questions that drive effective teaching and learning. She has crafted a powerful argument for why teachers must understand inquiry as a stance and then she shows teachers how to develop this stance as a foundation for their own self-directed, systematic, job-embedded professional learning. Digging Deeper Into Action Research *offers deeply grounded and inspiring support for teachers to learn from and with each other in the context of their everyday contributions to student learning."*

—Lauren Childs, Consultant for School Quality and Teacher Leadership
Oakland Schools, Waterford, MI

"Digging Deeper Into Action Research *can be used as both a trusted guide and as a provocateur. Educators need both as they develop an inquiry stance and embrace the complexity of teaching, with all its inherent tensions and dilemmas. Truly transformational learning—the kind that results in improved learning for students—requires that the learners will be transformed themselves. Engaging in the process of quality action research as described by Nancy Dana will lead to such transformation."*

—Gene Thompson-Grove, Education Consultant and Facilitator, Coach
The School Reform Initiative (SRI), Denver, CO

Digging DEEPER

A Teacher Inquirer's Field Guide

into Action Research

Nancy Fichtman Dana

Foreword by Marilyn Cochran-Smith

CORWIN
A SAGE Company

CORWIN
A SAGE Company

FOR INFORMATION:

Corwin

A SAGE Company

2455 Teller Road

Thousand Oaks, California 91320

(800) 233-9936

www.corwin.com

SAGE Publications Ltd.

1 Oliver's Yard

55 City Road

London EC1Y 1SP

United Kingdom

SAGE Publications India Pvt. Ltd.

B 1/I 1 Mohan Cooperative Industrial Area

Mathura Road, New Delhi 110 044

India

SAGE Publications Asia-Pacific Pte. Ltd.

3 Church Street

#10-04 Samsung Hub

Singapore 049483

Acquisitions Editor: Dan Alpert

Associate Editor: Kimberly Greenberg

Editorial Assistant: Heidi Arndt

Production Editor: Amy Schroller

Copy Editor: Codi Bowman

Typesetter: C&M Digitals (P) Ltd.

Proofreader: Wendy Jo Dymond

Indexer: Jean Casalegno

Cover Designer: Scott Van Atta

Permissions Editor: Karen Ehrmann

Copyright © 2013 by Corwin

Printed in the United States of America

A catalog record of this book is available from the Library of Congress.

ISBN 9781452241951

This book is printed on acid-free paper.

SUSTAINABLE FORESTRY INITIATIVE
Certified Chain of Custody
Promoting Sustainable Forestry
www.sfiprogram.org
SFI-01268
SFI label applies to text stock

13 14 15 16 17 10 9 8 7 6 5 4 3 2 1

Contents

List of Figures   vii

Foreword   ix

Preface   xiii

Acknowledgments   xvi

Introduction to the *Inspire to Inquire* DVD   xix

About the Author   xxii

How to Use the Inquiry Books   xxiii

1. **Why Do Teacher Research Anyway?**   1

   Teacher Research Defined   1
   How to Define Your Research   3
   Why It's Important: The 5 *E*s   4

2. **Developing and Fine-Tuning Your Wondering**   10

   Wondering Defined   10
   How to Define Your Wondering   11
   The Wondering Litmus Test   17

3. **Developing and Fine-Tuning Your Research Plan**   27

   Research Plan Defined   27
   How to Define Your Research Plan   28
   The Inquiry Plan Litmus Test   30

4. **Analyzing Your Data**   49

   Data Analysis Defined   49
   How to Avoid Data Analysis Paralysis   53
   The Data Analysis Litmus Test   57

5. **Presenting Your Research**   63

Presentation Defined   63
How to Define Your Presentation   64
The Presentation Litmus Test   70

6. **On Your Way: Teacher Research as
    a Way of Being in the World**   79

Inquiry Stance Defined   79
How to Define Your Stance   81
Living the Life of an Inquirer   85

References   87

Index   91

————————— ❧ —————————

Inspire to Inquire DVD Contents

1. **Introducing Inquiry**

2. **Inquiry as a Pathway to Understanding
   Teaching Strategies and Techniques**

3. **Inquiry as a Pathway to Equity**

4. **Inquiry as a Way of Being and Teaching**

5. **Inquiry and the Common Core**

6. **The Power and Passion of Inquiry**

List of Figures

1.1 The Inquiry Cycle   2

1.2 The 5 *E*s   5

3.1 Data Collection Brainstorm Chart   29

For all of the teacher inquirers I've had
the honor and privilege to work with through the years.

Foreword

It is now almost universally accepted that teacher quality is important and that teachers' work matters in school outcomes and the life chances of children and youth. There have been numerous scholarly and policy debates about how to define and measure teacher quality, and there have been multiple blueprints, commission reports, and research programs focused on how to improve teaching. Although all initiatives are grounded—either explicitly or implicitly—in certain governing assumptions about the nature of teaching, which may compete with or be inconsistent with the assumptions of other initiatives, there has not been nearly enough deliberate discussion about what kind of work teaching actually is and what kind of research might actually be used to make it better.

In this book, *Digging Deeper Into Action Research: A Teacher Inquirer's Field Guide,* which is a companion and complement to several previous books about action research, Nancy Fichtman Dana works from two explicit assumptions—that teaching is complex work and that research done by teachers and other practitioners is (at least part of) what is needed to improve teaching and learning. It's important to note that these assumptions are very different from the dominant viewpoint, which is reflected in policy initiatives such as Race to the Top and Our Future, Our Teachers, the Obama administration's blueprint for improving teacher preparation. In initiatives like these, the operating assumptions about teaching and learning are reductionist in that both teacher quality and students' learning are *equated with* high-stakes test scores. In my view, this simplistic equating of teacher quality with students' test scores is extremely problematic with far-reaching implications for teacher research, research on teaching, teacher education, professional development, teacher evaluation, and school reform.

A decade ago, I realized that, oddly enough, a book about writing—Anne Lamott's (1994) *Bird by Bird: Some Instructions on Writing and Life*—could be helpful in imagining and drawing attention to other ways of thinking about the nature of the work of teaching (Cochran-Smith, 2003). I pointed out in an editorial that Lamott advised writers to avoid simple oppositions in their writing; she said, "I used to think that paired opposites were a given, that love was the opposite of hate, right the opposite of wrong. But now I think we sometimes buy into these concepts because it is so much easier to embrace absolutes than to suffer reality. [Now] I don't think anything is the opposite of love. Reality is unforgivingly complex" (p. 104). It seemed to me that Lamott's writing advice and her ideas about the nature of reality could be instructive to our thinking about the nature of teaching if we really wanted to understand it and if we wanted to engage in research that had any chance of helping to improve it. So editing Lamott's phrase somewhat, I emphasized that *teaching* was unforgivingly complex, not simply good or bad, right or wrong, working or failing. Although absolutes and dichotomies like these were (and are) popular in headlines and campaign slogans, they're limited in their usefulness. They don't raise any questions about what it means to be engaged in the process of becoming an educated person in not only a democratic but also the global society or about whose knowledge and values are of most worth or what counts as evidence of the effectiveness of teaching and learning. They ignore all the nuances of "good" (or "bad") teaching of real students collected in actual classrooms at particular times and places and in fluid social, cultural, and political contexts within a long history of inequities in opportunities and outcomes.

Today, interestingly, many educational reformers and researchers acknowledge that teaching is complex and that there are enduring inequities, but they reach very different conclusions about what to do under these broad banners. For example, a June 2012 *Wall Street Journal* report on the "big issues" in education pitted Thomas Kane, the leader of the Gates Foundation's "Measures of Effective Teaching" project and a proponent of using test scores to evaluate teachers, against Linda Darling-Hammond, leader of the Stanford Center for Opportunity Policy in Education and an opponent of test scores for teacher evaluation. Kane said that because teaching is complex, the right approach to evaluating teachers is to combine student achievement gains with systematic classroom observations and student surveys. In other words, he argued that because teaching is so complex, we need multiple (and more) discrete pieces of evaluation to capture it. In contrast, Darling-Hammond said teaching is too complex to use student test scores for high-stakes decisions. She emphasized that scores are unreliable, they vary widely from year to year, and they measure too many things other than the effects of the teacher. Although it's clear that viewpoints like Kane's are dominant in current education policy and in much of the research about teaching and learning, it's worth noting that both of these viewpoints have research and other scholars and policy makers behind them.

One of my conclusions about all this is that we seem to have a language problem here. Actually, I think we have a lot more than a language problem, but language is one of the issues. Complexity theorists make a fundamental distinction between complicated and complex things. Complicated things may be highly sophisticated and have many parts, but the parts can be accurately and fully analyzed individually and apart from one another. And the relationships between the parts are highly stable and predictable. One theorist's examples of complicated systems (Cilliers, 1998) include jumbo jets and CD players, both of which can be given exact descriptions. In contrast, with complex things, which are also sophisticated and composed of many parts, complexity is manifested at the level of the thing itself. Complexity results from the interactions and nonlinear relationships of the parts and from intricate feedback loops in the system. Thus relationships are explicable, but not fully predictable. Examples here include the brain and social systems, neither of which can be reduced to the sum of its parts.

I believe that teaching-learning relationships are more akin to social systems than CD players, and I fear we will ultimately reach a dead end if we continue to measure, evaluate, and research teaching and learning *as if* they were pieces of a complicated machine. Happily, Nancy Dana's book works from the "teaching and learning as a social system" side of the street, rather than the CD player side. With the richer understanding of the nature of teaching that she uses in her book, it's clear that we need research that unpacks and reveals the complex and changing interrelationships of the teachers, students, families, colleagues, and communities that scaffold students' emerging understandings and knowledge. It's also clear that we need researchers who can get at the nuances of the work of teaching and learning by generating questions and systematically documenting practice from the inside.

The goal of Dana's field guide is to provide down-to-earth advice to teachers about doing action research. Her advice draws on her extensive experience in this area, both as an action researcher herself and as a teacher of others. Her advice takes the form of guiding principles, definitions, heuristics, and illustrations (some of which are in the form of video clips) to help teachers fine-tune their inquiries through deliberate and careful reflection on each phase of the process. In conclusion, Dana pulls all her advice together in the last chapter of the field guide, using our notion of "inquiry as stance" (Cochran-Smith & Lytle, 1999, 2009) as a larger set of ideas and frameworks in which to locate and embed her practical advice. In this way, she situates the everyday work of teacher research within the broader idea of inquiry stance, which is a theory of action that positions the collective intellectual capacity of teachers and other practitioners at the center of the transformation of teaching and learning in schools. From this perspective, inquiry is understood as a world view, a way of life, and a stance on the work of teaching that can guide and ground practitioners over the course of the professional lifespan.

This field guide will undoubtedly make a valuable contribution to the larger project of practitioners engaged in the work of reflecting on, studying, and interrogating their practice in order ultimately to improve the social life of classrooms and the learning opportunities and life chances of children.

—Marilyn Cochran-Smith

Cawthorne Professor of Teacher Education

Boston College

Preface

About This Book

After experiencing the power of practitioner inquiry as a part of my dissertation work where I engaged in collaborative action research with a group of teachers and their principal for an entire school year in 1991, I have been passionate about practitioner inquiry ever since. For the past 20 years, I have integrated inquiry into the fabric of initial teacher preparation in the professional development school; presented workshops, institutes, and various presentations on practitioner research to teachers and administrators in several states across the nation; initiated a program of action research in K–12 virtual schools; coached and studied principals engaged in inquiry as a way to gain insights into their administrative practice; directed a center for school improvement whose main goal was to support and promote practitioner research as a primary mechanism for school improvement across the state of Florida; created a website to support teachers in the inquiry process; and authored several books and research studies aimed at helping practitioners inquire into their practice. Across all of these inquiry endeavors, I have worked with hundreds of educators as they embarked on the inquiry journey.

Over time, I began to see patterns emerge in many teacher researchers' initial approaches to their work. These patterns encapsulated places where their initial work in each phase of the action research process might have been tweaked or massaged just a bit to lead to more powerful and deeper research efforts. I believed that if captured and placed in a succinct and useable form, teacher inquirers everywhere could learn from these patterns, dig deeper into their work, and ultimately produce higher quality research to improve life and learning conditions for teachers and students everywhere. This is why this book was written.

Who This Book Is For and How to Use It

While there exists a plethora of introductory texts on teacher research, this book takes off where other introductory texts on action research leave the reader, providing teacher inquirers tips for each part of the inquiry process as they are in the midst of doing it (i.e., developing a wondering, developing an inquiry plan, analyzing data, and presenting one's work). Hence, it serves as a perfect complement to books that introduce the process of practitioner inquiry, and coordinates seamlessly with the introductory text I authored with Diane Yendol-Hoppey, *The Reflective Educator's Guide to Classroom Research.* Yet this book can also be used as a short, succinct, stand-alone text to guide teachers through the inquiry process in a very targeted and specific way. Teachers can use this text to get jump-started in the process for the first time and can refer to lengthier texts on the subject later to learn more detail about the process.

Many preservice teachers engage in inquiry as a part of their teacher education programs at various times and in various configurations. In addition, many practicing teachers engage in inquiry as a part of advanced graduate study at the university. Sometimes course work for preservice teachers and graduate students focuses specifically on action research, and at other times, action research is undertaken as an assignment in a content or methods course, such as Teaching Children Mathematics. This book may be used as a text in any university course (whether or not the course focuses on action research) to scaffold assignments related to inquiry that may be a part of the class syllabus. Its short length enables the text to be used in content courses without overwhelming the student, and as a complement to other readings on practitioner research, it will help students enrolled in courses on action research produce higher quality final projects.

In addition to being a valuable resource for practicing teachers to supplement other lengthier texts or jump-start them in the process of inquiry as professional development and college students to help them craft higher quality research as a part of coursework, this book is also for any educator who coaches action research. In essence, the book itself serves as an action research coach. It is a brief resource coaches can give to their coachees to provide them with a checklist of sorts as they progress through each phase of the inquiry process, making the complex job of the inquiry coach easier.

The goal of this book is to help teachers fine-tune their work and ultimately produce higher quality research than would be produced in the absence of deliberate reflection on and careful scrutiny of each phase in the action research cycle: developing a wondering, developing a research plan, analyzing data, and presenting the research. If you are a teacher researcher, this book can serve as a critical friend, gently pushing you a little further in each step of the process. And if we all push ourselves a little deeper in the inquiry process, we capitalize on the capacity of teacher research to raise teacher voice in educational reform and improve schooling for all children. Happy inquiring!

Acknowledgments

There is nothing I am more grateful for in my professional career than the opportunities I have had to meet and work alongside incredible teacher inquirers through the classes I have taught on practitioner research at the University as well as workshops and institutes I have conducted on the topic throughout the nation. While it would be impossible to name all of the passionate teacher researchers who have touched my professional life, I dedicate this book to each of you, with gratitude for all I have learned about the process through you. In particular, I thank the following teacher and administrator researchers for allowing me to feature their work and/or their words in this book so that others can be inspired to inquire: Jamey Burns, Steve Burgin, Gary Boulware, Kathy Christensen, Brooke Cobbin, Darby Delane, Sharon Earle, Debbi Hubbell, Angela Jackson, Karen Mallory, Cheryl Quarles-Gaston, Thea Saccasyn, May Steward, Tracy Staley, Marisa Stukey, Sherif Watson, Stephanie Whitaker, and Rachel Wolkenhauer.

I have been incredibly fortunate to be working with the Lastinger Center for Learning in the College of Education at the University of Florida for the past several years. Lastinger Center Director Don Pemberton has done a remarkable job of building capacity for inquiry by embedding the concept into the fabric of the work done by this Center. Of particular note are the partnerships he built with four of the largest school districts in our state, empowering teachers who work within high-need, high-poverty schools to use the process of inquiry to make life and learning conditions better for the children they teach. These teachers' work has been supported by Lastinger Center Inquiry Leaders: Jamey Burns, Kathy Christensen, Kathy Dixon, Lauren Gibbs, Valerie Mendez-Farinas, Josette Paris, Kaethe Perez, Janice Schomburg, Carolyn Spillman, Shirley Rainwaters, Alex Prinstein, Vicki Vescio, and Liz Young. Much of the material for this book was derived from inquiry leader retreats we had over the past two years as we worked together to better understand the ways the inquiry process was playing out for these teachers and how we could better support and scaffold their research. The expert video production talents of Lastinger Center's Boaz Dvir enabled us to capture many of these teacher researchers in action. I am grateful to Don, Boaz, the Lastinger inquiry leaders, and the entire Lastinger Center staff for their tireless efforts to empower teachers (and the students they teach) through inquiry.

Inquiry has become a signature feature of three teacher education programs at the University of Florida (UF)—ProTeach, The Teacher Leadership for School Improvement Program (TLSI), and the Curriculum, Teaching, and Teacher Education (CTTE) Professional Practice Doctorate. I thank my colleagues in each of these programs for their commitment to approaching inquiry not as one assignment to be completed by our students, but as a critical stance we wish to cultivate in our students to serve them well throughout their professional lifetimes. Hence, rather than practitioner inquiry being encapsulated in one course and one experience, inquiry permeates the entirety of these programs. Alyson Adams, Buffy Bondy, Magdi Castaneda, Raquel Diaz, Darby Delane, Tanetha Grosland, Ruth Lowery, Brianna Kennedy-Lewis, Phil Poekert, Rose Pringle, Dorene Ross, Joy Schackow, Carolyn Spillman, Colleen Swain, Crystal Timmons, Vicki Vescio—I thank you for your colleagueship and your camaraderie in helping UF preservice teachers, practicing teachers, and doctoral students take an inquiry stance toward their teaching.

My work on inquiry has been greatly influenced by Gene Thompson-Grove and the School Reform Initiative (SRI), an organization that creates transformational learning communities fiercely committed to educational equity and excellence (www.schoolreform initiative.org/). Gene introduced me to protocols and I have both used and adapted many of the protocols developed by SRI in my inquiry coaching work with powerful results. I thank Gene and SRI for the foundation they have provided for educators to become deeply reflective professionals who take an inquiry stance toward teaching and learning.

My very best friends and closest colleagues are my family—my husband, Tom, and my young adult children, Greg and Kirsten. They have always wrapped my writing projects in the love and support needed to see a project through. Thank you for continuing to provide the foundation for the writing of a book to unfold.

Finally, I thank my former editor Carol Collins and current editor Dan Alpert. Carol provided ongoing support for this work as it was being conceptualized and throughout the beginning of the project and worked her editing magic to bring brilliant ideas to life within this text and the DVD that accompanies it. Dan provided fresh eyes and enthusiasm to this piece in the homestretch of the writing. Thank you both for your energy and support in bringing this text from idea to reality.

Publisher's Acknowledgments

Corwin gratefully acknowledges the contributions of the following reviewers:

Mary K. Culver
Associate Clinical Professor
Northern Arizona University
Flagstaff, AZ

Helen Kloepper
Instructional Coach
USD 230, Spring Hill Intermediate School
Spring Hill, KS

Jana Scott Lindsay
Educational Consultant–Curriculum and Instruction
Saskatoon Public Schools
Canada

Gail V. Ritchie
Instructional Coach
Fairfax County Public Schools
Centreville, VA

Jennifer L. Snow
Professor and Teacher Education Coordinator
Boise State University
Boise, ID

Introducing the *Inspire to Inquire* DVD

In sum, the text of this book is designed to help teachers fine-tune their work throughout each phase of the inquiry cycle. While each chapter includes many examples of teacher researchers' work to accomplish this task, there is no substitute for actually seeing and hearing real teacher researchers in action. For this reason, a unique feature of the book is the accompanying *Inspire to Inquire* DVD.

The *Inspire to Inquire* DVD contains four short video clips that cut across the book as a whole and provide stories of practitioner inquirers and the importance of the work they do. Two additional clips enable the reader to meet the author in person to learn more about her work with inquiry throughout the years and her passion for the process.

The clips are designed to ignite discussion about the inquiry process and the power it holds to transform teaching and learning in classrooms and schools across the nation. As such, a great way to use these clips is at venues, such as faculty meetings, professional development workshops, or college classes. Each clip can kickoff a meeting, workshop, or college class by serving as a springboard for discussion about the inquiry process and each teacher's inquiry work. The video clips can also extend face-to-face faculty meeting, workshop, or college class meeting time by serving as an impetus for online discussions of the clip's content in between work sessions that focus on each phase of the inquiry cycle: developing a wondering, developing a research plan, analyzing data, and presenting the research.

Finally, clips can also be viewed by individuals at various times as they progress through the content of this book to provide inspiration and ideas for the ways the processes described in the text translate into real classroom and school contexts.

Clip 1, titled **Introducing Inquiry**, provides a brief overview of the entire inquiry process and its importance by author Nancy Fichtman Dana. As such, it's a great clip to view before even beginning the text or as a complement to Chapter 1. This clip can serve as a catalyst for the book and the inquiry process itself and the ways both might be used to further school improvement and professional development endeavors in a district or school or further one's learning about teaching as an education student in a college or university.

Clip 2, titled **Inquiry as a Pathway to Understanding Teaching Strategies and Techniques**, features teacher inquirer Tracy Staley. Tracy teaches fifth-grade science in a Title One school where approximately 75% of the students are on free or reduced-price lunch. Discouraged by her students' performance on her state's standardized reading and science tests, Tracy wished to try some new approaches to the teaching of science and wondered, "What is the relationship between my students' participation in station activity and their science learning?" This clip chronicles Tracy's use of the inquiry process to gain insights into the implementation of her new approach to the organization of her science instruction and the impact it had on her students' learning.

Clip 3, titled **Inquiry as a Pathway to Equity**, features high school social studies teacher Gary Boulware, who engaged in inquiry to increase access to the AP courses he taught after noticing that his classes were occupied mostly by white, upper-middle-class students, and Thea Saccasyn, a principal who led her entire faculty in inquiry to uncover and challenge their assumptions and biases related to the children they teach in her high-need, high-poverty school. This clip portrays the promise the inquiry movement holds to create more equitable classrooms for our children and youth.

Clip 4, titled **Inquiry as a Way of Being and Teaching**, features **ESOL** teacher Stephanie Whitaker. This clip portrays the way Stephanie uses the inquiry process to approach her mathematics instruction, teaching for conceptual understanding rather than procedural understanding of the mathematics concepts covered in her curriculum with outstanding results.

Clip 5, titled **Inquiry and the Common Core**, features educational consultant Jamey Burns and the work she has done with one elementary school to use the process of inquiry as a mechanism to better

Wilson Fellows

understand the Common Core as it rolls out in their district. An interesting component of this DVD clip is the introduction it provides to student inquiry, applying the same process that teachers use to learn more about their professional practice to students in the classroom. This clip portrays the promise engaging students in inquiry holds to actualize the Common Core in classrooms.

Serving as the final clip on the DVD, Clip 6, titled **The Power and Passion of Inquiry**, again features author Nancy Fichtman Dana reflecting on the process of inquiry as a whole and the importance of taking an inquiry stance toward one's teaching. As such, it's a great clip to view after completing the text or as a complement to Chapter 6. This clip can serve to bring closure to the completion of one cycle of inquiry as explicated in the book, and it might even be viewed at the end of an Inquiry Showcase where teachers in a school or district have presented their work to one another or university students have presented an inquiry they've completed during the semester to their classmates and the instructor at the final class of the semester. The purpose of this clip is to inspire inquirers to continue their research. Hence, this clip might also be used at a faculty meeting or district workshop designed to help teachers reflect on and evaluate the inquiry work they've just completed during one school year and provide the impetus for teachers to plan their next cycle of inquiry by answering questions such as "Where do we wish to take our research next?" and "What new wonderings do we have?"

However you choose to use the clips contained on the DVD, the clips help the words contained in the following pages of this book come alive in unique and interesting ways. The intended result of viewing these clips in combination with the reading of the text is to help the reader inspire to inquire and continue one's inquiry journey throughout the professional lifetime. Enjoy each clip. Enjoy the journey. Bon voyage!

About the Author

 **Nancy Fichtman Dana** is currently Professor of Education in the School of Teaching and Learning at the University of Florida, Gainesville, and has been studying practitioner inquiry for the last twenty years. During this time, she has developed and taught classes on practitioner research for undergraduate, masters, and doctoral students; coached the practitioner research of numerous educators from various districts across the nation; as well as published seven books and more than 50 book chapters and articles in professional journals focused on teacher and principal professional development and practitioner inquiry.

How to Use the Inquiry Books

This table summarizes the books I have authored or coauthored related to inquiry and describes their focus, differentiating the texts and delineating their use.

Book	Authors	Focus
The Reflective Educator's Guide to Classroom Research: Learning to Teach and Teaching to Learn through Practitioner Inquiry (2009) (Facilitator's Guide Available)	Nancy Fichtman Dana, Diane Yendol-Hoppey	This book provides an in-depth introduction to teacher inquiry for both prospective and practicing teachers, taking the reader step by step through the process including developing a wondering, collaborating with others, collecting data, analyzing data, writing up one's work, assessing the quality of inquiry, and sharing one's work with others. A great first book on teacher inquiry.
The Reflective Educator's Guide to Professional Development: Coaching Inquiry-Oriented Learning Communities (2008)	Nancy Fichtman Dana, Diane Yendol-Hoppey	This book focuses on coaching the inquiry process within professional learning communities. In addition to tips on the establishment of healthy learning communities, it contains numerous coaching resources to take teachers through each stage of the inquiry process.
Leading with Passion and Knowledge: The Principal as Action Researcher (2009)	Nancy Fichtman Dana	This book takes administrators through the step-by-step process of inquiry, offering rich examples of principals engaged in each step of the process. This is a perfect resource for districts to provide powerful professional development for principals as well as

(Continued)

(Continued)

Book	Authors	Focus
		university professors to help their students enrolled in educational leadership programs write an action research thesis or dissertation.
Powerful Professional Development: Building Expertise within the Four Walls of Your School (2010)	Diane Yendol-Hoppey, Nancy Fichtman Dana	This book provides a bird's-eye view of numerous job-embedded professional development strategies. In addition to a chapter on inquiry, chapters focus on book studies, webinars and podcasts, coteaching, conversation tools, lesson study, culturally responsive and content focused coaching, and professional learning communities.
Inquiry: A Districtwide Approach to Staff and Student Learning (2011)	Nancy Fichtman Dana, Carol Thomas, Sylvia Boynton	This book describes the ways engagement in inquiry fits together for all constituencies within a district—principals, teachers, students, and coaches. This systems overview of inquiry and the ways the process can connect improved practice to student achievement enables the reader to enhance learning for adults and students across an entire district.
Digging Deeper into Action Research: A Teacher Inquirer's Field Guide (2012)	Nancy Fichtman Dana	This book takes off where other introductory texts on action research leave the reader, providing teacher inquirers tips for each part of the inquiry process as they are in the midst of doing it (i.e., developing a wondering, developing an inquiry plan, analyzing data, and presenting one's work). A perfect complement to *The Reflective Educator's Guide to Classroom Research*, but it can also be used as a short, succinct, stand-alone text to guide teachers through the inquiry process in a very targeted and specific way. It may also be used as a text in any university course (whether or not the course focuses on action research), to help students complete a required inquiry-based assignment.

1

Why Do Teacher Research Anyway?

Teacher research is exhilarating to the educator because it respects their wisdom and gives them an active voice in improving practice. Through inquiry, teachers leave their footprints in the problem-solving process.

—Sherif A. Watson, Teacher Inquirer,
Santa Clara Elementary School

Teacher Research Defined

Tracing its roots to the work of John Dewey (1933), the concept "practitioners as researchers" that was popularized by Kurt Lewin in the 1940s (Adelman, 1993), and shortly thereafter applied to the field of education by Stephen Corey (1953), has been around for decades. Since its inception, many educational innovations have come and gone, but the systematic study of teachers' practice is a concept that has proved its staying power.

Because the concept of teacher research originated years ago and has endured through time, it is not surprising that multiple models, iterations, and even names for the process have emerged through the years and have been actualized in varying ways for varying purposes (Somekh & Zeichner, 2009). "Teacher research," "action research," "classroom research," "practitioner inquiry," "teacher inquiry," and "teacher self-study" are all names that are often used interchangeably throughout the nation, despite some differences in historical evolution and theoretical grounding of these versions of and variance in the practitioner research process (Cochran-Smith & Lytle, 2009).

While versions and variance exist, in general, teacher research is defined simply as systematic, intentional study of one's professional practice (see Cochran-Smith & Lytle, 1993, 2009). Inquiring professionals seek change by reflecting on their practice. As illustrated in Figure 1.1, they do this by engaging in a cyclical process of posing questions or "wonderings," collecting data to gain insights into their wonderings, analyzing the data along with reading relevant literature, taking action to make changes in practice based on new understandings developed during inquiry, and sharing findings with others (Dana & Yendol-Hoppey, 2009). This model of inquiry, found particularly useful to scaffold powerful job-embedded learning for educators (Dana, Thomas, & Boynton, 2011; Yendol-Hoppey & Dana, 2010) as well as support the learning of new teachers as they prepare to enter the profession (Dana & Silva, 2001; Dana, Silva, & Gerono, 2002) is the focus of this book.

Figure 1.1   The Inquiry Circle

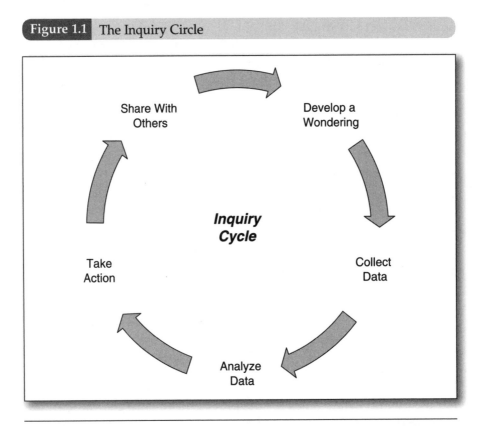

Source: Dana, Thomas, and Boynton (2011). *Inquiry: A Districtwide Approach to Staff and Student Learning.* Thousand Oaks, CA: Corwin. Reprinted by permission.

How to Define Your Research

Defining your research begins simply with careful and critical reflection on your teaching practice. Because the acts of teaching and learning are inherently complex endeavors, there are many aspects of your practice that might spur great practitioner research.

For example, you might begin to define your research through reflection on each of the students you teach individually. Which of your students are puzzling to you for some reason?

- Perhaps a particular learner or group of leaners is struggling to understand the content you are teaching.
- Perhaps a particular learner or group of learners is not behaving in ways that are conducive to your classroom environment.
- Perhaps a particular learner or group of learners are advanced academically and have already mastered the curriculum you are charged with teaching this year.
- Perhaps a particular learner or group of learners come to school hungry, without basic health care, and other needs not being met making school a challenging place to be.

Reflection on individual learners is a great way to begin to shape ideas for your classroom-based research.

Alternatively, you might begin to define your research through reflection on your curriculum.

- What aspects of your curriculum are most and least comfortable for you to teach and why?
- What aspects of your curriculum are most and least connected to the lived experiences of your students?
- Which aspects of your curriculum are most and least challenging for your students to understand?
- For what type of learner is your curriculum designed?
- Who benefits from your curriculum?
- Who doesn't?

Reflection on curriculum is another fine way to begin to shape ideas for your classroom-based research.

A final way you might begin to define your research is through reflection on teaching strategies or techniques that you wish to try in your classroom to achieve a particular purpose or goal.

- What are these strategies?
- What is known about them?

- Which of your learners might these strategies serve best?
- Which of your learners might these strategies serve least?

Reflection on pedagogy can also inspire ideas for classroom-based research.

These areas for focused reflection (individual learners, curriculum, teaching strategies/techniques) are just a few of many paths you might consider taking as you formulate your research. While reflection provides a generic framing for the formation of a classroom-based inquiry, your research develops greater definition as you progress through each phase of the process—developing your wondering, developing a research plan, collecting and analyzing data, and sharing your work with others.

This book is designed to take you through each of these critical junctures in the practitioner inquiry process in a succinct and targeted way to help you define and refine a personally meaningful and powerful piece of practitioner research as you are in the midst of doing it. Before you begin the act of action research in Chapters 2 through 5, however, it's important to develop a firm foundation for why it's important to engage in the practitioner inquiry process in the first place.

Why It's Important: The 5 *E*s

While practitioner research has been around for decades, it has taken on increased importance in contemporary times since the introduction of No Child Left Behind (NCLB) and the subsequent emphasis on high-stakes testing and accountability. According to leading scholars on the practitioner research movement Marilyn Cochran-Smith and Susan Lytle (2009),

> NCLB has narrowed the meaning of teaching and is having severe effects on teachers and student learning. We believe NCLB's conception of teaching and learning are flawed— linear, remarkably narrow, and based on a technical transmission model of teaching, learning, and teacher training that was rejected more than 2 decades ago and that is decidedly out of keeping with contemporary understandings of learning. Like it or not, diverse stakeholders in the educational process are coming to regard teachers as technicians, student learning as test performance, and teacher learning as training about "what works." To improve student learning and to

retain qualified teachers, we need to unpack and critique the images of teachers and teaching that are creeping into the national psyche. (pp. 62, 82–83)

Engagement in practitioner research is one way to trouble the images held by the education community, the policy community, and the public that have been shaped by NCLB and subsequent national dialogue about the state of education, images that are antithetical to "the importance of local knowledge and the idea that teachers and other practitioners have the capacity to generate local knowledge of practice through their own classroom and school inquiries" (Cochran-Smith & Lytle, p. 68). Today, political attacks on education and educators continue and are becoming more frequent and more severe. Figure 1.2 titled The 5 Es serves as a mnemonic device to inspire you to engage in your research and energize you throughout each step of the process, particularly in these trying education times.

The 5 *E*s

The first *E* word found in Figure 1.2 is "Engage." There is a great deal of educational rhetoric these days about the importance of student engagement. According to engagement expert Phillip Schlechty (2011),

Figure 1.2   The 5 *E*s

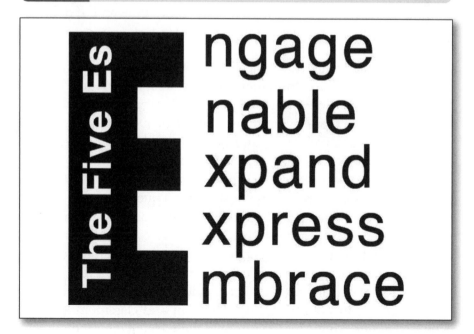

student engagement is characterized by four components. The engaged student is attentive, committed, persistent, and "finds meaning and value in the tasks that make up the work" (p. 14).

On the surface, the fact that student engagement is receiving increased attention and is touted as a valued outcome of school reform might appear somewhat silly. Of course, teachers strive on a daily basis to engage every student in learning. Do you know any classroom teacher who aspires to a classroom full of *dis*engaged learners?

Yet perhaps student engagement is receiving heightened attention in the literature as achieving student engagement becomes increasingly difficult in the darkness of the current educational landscape where some outside the field of education are attacking teachers, administrators, students, and the entire public schooling enterprise. Those who are speaking critically about the field of education believe that the complex processes of teaching and learning can be reduced to a simple test score. This myopic focus on test scores makes creating engaging learning contexts more and more difficult for teachers. Schlechty (2011) laments,

> As things now stand, many teachers with whom I work comment that although they would like to give their students more engaging work and would enjoy teaching more if they could spend time designing such work, they have standardized tests to worry about and therefore cannot afford to spend time on designing engaging work for students, even it if does produce more profound learning. (p. 38)

The fact that the high-stakes testing environment creates conditions that are not conducive to student engagement means that teacher engagement in inquiry is more important than ever. Through *engaging* in inquiry during these trying times, you create a classroom environment that is qualitatively different from what goes on in a test-driven-only classroom. Researching teachers create school and classroom environments in which there are researching students. Students and teacher work together to ask (not just answer) questions, and to pose (not just solve) problems. By becoming question-askers and problem-posers, students and teachers work together to construct curriculum from their context and lived experiences, rather than just receive preselected and predigested information that will appear on a test. And in working to construct meaningful curriculum together, you and your students *engage* in professional development and classroom learning activity that offers hope for the future in these trying education times.

Cochran-Smith and Lytle (2009) write that

There are critical relationships between teacher learning and student learning. When teachers learn differently, students learn differently; when teachers at all levels or experience are encouraged to ask questions, their students are more likely to find themselves in classrooms where their own questions, not rote answers, signal active and consequential engagement with ideas. In our troubled democracy, there is no more significant outcome for educational institutions, and we cannot afford to cultivate an image of teachers and teaching that promises less. (p. 85)

As an inquirer, then, you have the power to push back against a test-driven only view of teaching and learning, and *engage* every student you teach.

The second *E* word found in figure 1.2 is "Enable." A wonderful benefit of inquiry is that through your work as an inquirer and the sharing of that work with others, you *enable* others to learn from you! As a teacher, you have already touched the lives of countless children who have occupied the four walls of your classrooms and your schools. Through engagement in inquiry, you make a difference in the lives of many more children you will never teach and never even meet—the children of other practitioners who benefit from inquiring beside you, hearing you discuss the learning that has taken place through the process of inquiry, and the subsequent improvements they make based on what they've learned from you. As an inquirer, you *enable* powerful learning not only for the children *you* teach, but also for your adult colleagues as well!

The third *E* word found in Figure 1.2 is "Expand." Through inquiry, you *expand* the knowledge base for teaching and learning. When we turn back the pages on the history of educational research, for many years, research on teaching and learning in education was conducted by what was referred to as "outside experts," mostly university researchers who were removed from the daily life of classrooms (Cochran-Smith & Lytle, 1993). While valuable knowledge was produced during these years, it has become evident that when research on teaching and learning in education is produced only by those outside the classroom, a gaping hole in knowledge about teaching exists, for those who are closest to children, practitioners, are uniquely positioned to study teaching and generate critical knowledge from within the four walls of their classrooms and schools. Through your work as an inquirer, you make immense contributions to the literature and the field, expanding what we know and need to find out about the complex processes of teaching and learning. Through inquiry, you put theory into practice and practice into theory, supplementing the study of teaching from the outside–in with valuable insights that only those who work closest with children can generate from the inside–out. As an inquirer, you *expand* all that is known, and what we can know, about the wonderful world of teaching and learning.

The fourth *E* word in Figure 1.2 is "Express." Research tells us that an important quality of exemplary teachers is that who they are as teachers and who they are as people are intricately intertwined. For example, in a seminal case study of six exemplary teachers, it was concluded that

> Teaching as identity is the clearest theme to emerge in this study, and teaching as identity is the frame through which each of these case studies makes sense. In these cases, there is no clear line delineating the person and the teacher. Rather, there is a seamless web between teaching and being, between teacher and person. Teaching is not simply what one does, it is who one is. (Ayers, 1989, p. 130)

Hence, in this great profession of teaching, your personal and professional identities intersect and merge with one another, creating the unique being and teacher that is you. In the wake of increasing federal and state standardization of the act of teaching characterized by such things as rigid adherence to pacing guides and other forces working to mold all teachers into one cookie-cutter image, inquiry allows you to *express* your unique identity as teacher, *your* individual being. Through wondering aloud with other teacher professionals, you reclaim your unique and individual teacher identity. You *express* who you are, and you are empowered to do the very best you can, to work in the very best interest of every student you teach. As an inquirer, you *express* all that is unique and wonderful about being an educator.

The fifth and final *E* word found in Figure 1.2 is "Embrace." By doing inquiry, you reject the notion that teaching is a simple endeavor and celebrate all the great complexity inherent in the act of teaching itself. Now, because there is a great deal of complexity inherent in teaching, it is natural and normal for many issues, tensions, problems, and dilemmas to emerge. Rather than sweeping these under the carpet and pretending they don't exist, through the act of inquiry, you *embrace* problems, and regard them not as an educator's foe but as an educator's friend. Through embracing problems of practice, you demonstrate that inquiry is less about what one does (one action research project completed at one point in time) and more about who one is (a teacher who positions him or herself professionally not as an implementer of a rigid, unchanging teaching routine year after year, but a constant and continuous questioner, wonderer, and explorer throughout the professional lifetime). Embracing problems means that inquiry is not about solving every educational problem that exists—given the complexity of teaching and learning, that would be impossible. Rather, engaging in inquiry is about finding new and better problems to study, and in so doing, leading a continuous cycle of self and school improvement—truly, becoming the best that you can be. This important professional positioning is called an inquiry stance. As an inquirer, you *embrace* this stance and allow it to rest at the core of your professional being. We'll return to the concept of inquiry stance in the final chapter of this book.

The 5 *E*s were presented in this chapter to help you reflect on the importance of the work you do as a teacher, and as an inquirer, each and every day. Unfortunately, at some point in their careers, teachers come across the adage

"Those who can, do. Those who can't, teach."

Regrettably, this fairly common saying reflects a society that doesn't understand, appreciate, or value the work of a teacher. The 5 *E*s figure shared in this chapter is a reminder that engagement in the process of inquiry provides the opportunity for teachers to be recognized in meaningful ways as a professional. This, in turn, helps to replace that terribly inaccurate adage with a new one:

"Those who can, teach.

Those who can't, find some other, less important profession."

Through engagement in inquiry, you bring your teaching to life. You become an advocate not only for the children you teach, but for the teaching profession itself. So let the process begin with the development and refinement of your research question in Chapter 2.

2

Developing and Fine-Tuning Your Wondering

Wonderings are like planning for a grand adventure: You may not know yet where you're going or how you're going to get there— but you know it will be memorable and impact you and others.

—Kathy Christensen, Teacher Inquirer,
Village Oaks Elementary School

Wondering Defined

A wondering is defined as a burning question a teacher has about his practice. While many models of action research simply use the straightforward term *question*, in my work, I have used the term *wondering* to emphasize the inviting nature of inquiry for the teacher researcher. As shared in Chapter 1, because the act of teaching is so complex, it is natural and normal for many issues, tensions, problems, and dilemmas to emerge each and every day a teacher walks through the classroom doors, and therefore, it is natural and normal for teachers to *wonder* everyday about their practice. Wonder is the foundation for formulating a researchable question based on issues, tensions, problems, or dilemmas experienced by the teacher. According to Michael Fullan (1993), "Problems are our friends." Rather than bemoan problems or sweep them under the carpet and pretend they don't exist, teacher inquirers embrace problems by naming them and carefully shaping them into a researchable question. Table 2.1 (see pp. 12–14) contains examples of wonderings explored by several individual and groups of teacher researchers.

How to Define Your Wondering

To define your wondering, begin by exploring, articulating, and reflecting on your "friends," problems of practice that create tensions or cause dilemmas in your work as a classroom teacher. There are three great strategies a teacher researcher can use to explore, articulate, and reflect: talking, brainstorming, and reading.

Talking. As teachers, we talk all the time. We talk to our students, we talk to our colleagues, we talk to parents, we talk to administrators, and often, to debrief our busy days in the classroom, we talk to friends, and we talk to family. The talk we do serves many purposes, and one very productive purpose it can serve is to help us give voice to our passions, challenges, frustrations, fears, hopes, joys, and dreams. These are the ingredients that good wonderings are made of!

One potential pitfall of teacher talk is negativity. Because teaching is such a complicated endeavor, it is, consequently, full of challenges, and these challenges can easily turn faculty room and parking lot talk into unproductive venting and complaining sessions. While everyone needs a good venting space from time to time, teacher researchers know that, ultimately, venting and complaining are not actions that lead to the productive outcomes that inquiry can bring. Rather, teacher researchers dig deep into their professional being to unearth aspects of teaching that cause them discomfort or unease and seek to do something about it. Kettering refers to research essentially as "Nothing but a state of mind . . . a friendly, welcoming attitude towards change . . . going out to look for change instead of waiting for it to come" (as quoted in Boyd, 1961). This mind-set serves as the foundation for transforming the talk of teaching into productive wonderings.

So if you have ever engaged in talk about your teaching with others, you are already on the road to developing a wondering. Continue the

Table 2.1   50 Examples of Wonderings by Grade Level and Teaching Area

Elementary (K–5):	
Math	• How does one teach fractions conceptually, and what are the impacts of that teaching on the different learners in my classroom? • What is the relationship between students' basic math fact fluency and their ability to problem solve? • How can I differentiate instruction and use our district's adopted math program?
Language Arts	• What is the best way to use a word wall? • What is the relationship between the reading of fractured fairytale plays and the fluency development of fourth graders?
Science	• How can I encourage students to use scientific terms when talking about science? • How do online demonstrations compare to live demonstrations regarding effectiveness in capturing students' interest? • How can I take a science unit that is heavy on content and make it more inquiry based?
Social Studies	• How can the story of the true discovery of America be taught to fourth graders in a developmentally appropriate way? • How will the implementation of the organizational structure embedded in interactive notebooks help our students understand the scientific process and gain historical perspectives in social studies? • How will using role play and simulations increase student understanding of historical events? • How do I begin to engage students in discussing difficult and controversial issues?
Secondary (6–12)	
Math	• How does the use of tessellations as a context for students to investigate geometric shapes and their properties play out in my classroom? • How can I instill in my seventh graders a habit of working through math problems on multiple choice tests so they do well on our state standardized test?
Language Arts	• What happens when I put culturally relevant literature in the hands of my eighth-grade reluctant readers? • How will the use of comprehension strategies effect student reading achievement in the area of vocabulary? • What are some strategies I could use to facilitate better literature discussions?
Science	• How can I better use demonstrations in a way that empowers my students' learning of high school chemistry? • What is the relationship between investigations I typically use and my students' developing understandings of Bernoulli's Principle?

Social Studies	• How does using technology such as Google Earth impact students' understanding and application of geography skills? • How will deepening my adult content knowledge and understandings about the Holocaust translate into the ways I teach this topic?
Special Areas	
Art	• How can still life drawing help children see multiple perspectives and apply this to social situations? • What is the relationship between students' expressing themselves through art and their writing for language arts assignments?
Music	• Which music and movement techniques can help improve my students' behavior during large-group/circle time? • How can I teach music theory in a performance-oriented class? • How might music help a particular student combat some frustrations when reading and boost her self-esteem?
Foreign Language	• In what ways can I improve my students' ability to write in French? • How does keeping a daily, personal journal help Spanish students improve written grammar?
Physical Education	• What are the best ways to grade students in physical education class? • In what ways can physical education activities build on students' learning to read in kindergarten and first grade?
Technology Education	• How can a team of teachers work through problems together and support one another overcome hurdles when using new technologies? • How can the use of assistive technologies (AlphaSmart, Kidspiration, audio recordings, and Stationary Studio) increase the writing quality, interest, and motivation for a gifted third-grade student? • How can I use a SMART board to best facilitate student learning?
Administration	• What are teachers' levels of satisfaction with the current block schedule in place at the secondary level? • What are viable alternatives to ISS (in-school suspension) and how do they play out in our high school? • What are some strategies for promoting teacher leadership in my school, and how are they working? • In what ways does peer coaching contribute to the continued professional development of veteran teachers, and what role can I play as a principal to facilitate the process?
Generic Act of Teaching (K–12)	
	• How can I better communicate with my middle school students' parents? • What are the most effective methods to ensure that show and tell is a meaningful, academic-related activity?

(Continued)

| Table 2.1 | (Continued) |

	<ul><li>How do I design an extension of the reciprocal teaching method that is both effective and efficient while still engaging to students?</li><li>How can I incorporate more higher level questions into classroom discussions and have students recognize and answer them as such?</li><li>How can we make inclusion meetings more helpful for students and educators in our school?</li><li>What impact will a critical friends group have on the teaching and professional growth of members of the group?</li><li>How can students be taught organizational skills and strategies so they will use them to improve their academic performance?</li><li>How do the structure and management of my classroom effect a particular student's behavior?</li><li>How does my questioning behavior change as I teach across subjects?</li><li>How can I use my students' social skills to enhance their learning and instruction at the same time?</li><li>How do the ways I phrase questions contribute to how learners interpret them?</li><li>In what ways do my classroom management and practices deter from my philosophy of teaching and my beliefs about how children learn?</li><li>How can I maintain an inclusive classroom when high-stakes testing seems to encourage noninclusive practices?</li></ul>

Source: Dana & Yendol-Hoppey (2008). *The Reflective Educator's Guide to Professional Development: Coaching Inquiry-Oriented Learning Communities.* Thousand Oaks, CA: Corwin. Reprinted by permission.

process of talk while simultaneously guarding against it becoming simple venting or complaining time. Some questions that might help to frame talk in productive ways to give rise to good wonderings are the following:

- What do you believe to be your greatest teaching strength and your greatest area for improvement in your teaching?
- Which of your students are most puzzling to you and why?
- What about your curriculum do you find the most challenging to teach? Why?
- What innovative teaching strategies have you heard or read about that you'd like to try?
- What innovations have you recently introduced into your teaching practice that do not appear to be working in the ways you had hoped?

- What are your students' scores on standardized tests and other assessment measures your district uses telling you about the learning needs of your students?
- What recent district, state, and federal mandates are you working to translate into practice and how is it going?
- What inspires you in your teaching practice, and what causes your enthusiasm to wane?
- What do you imagine to be different in your classroom? Your school? Your district?
- What keeps you awake at night, or what are you thinking about on your drive to work?
- What's the one thing in education that you'd most like to change and why?

These questions serve as great research conversation starters.

Brainstorming. Talk opens up all kinds of possibilities for research. Using talk as the impetus for the specific act of brainstorming allows teacher researchers to give voice to an array of possibilities for exploration through inquiry and to subsequently assess each possibility's potential value to their teaching and their students' learning. As the relative value of exploring different wonderings is assessed, teacher researchers narrow the possibilities for their research and, ultimately, settle on one direction or topic for inquiry.

Reading. As teacher researchers talk, brainstorm, and consider possibilities for their research, many also find inspiration for their wonderings by reading the work of other teacher researchers. Fortunately, teacher research is fairly easy to come by. Many collections of teacher research have been published, such as *Creating Equitable Classrooms Through Action Research* (Caro-Bruce, Flessner, Klehr, & Zeichner, 2007), *Taking Action With Teacher Research* (Meyers & Rust, 2003), and *Empowering the Voice of the Teacher Researcher: Achieving Success through a Culture of Inquiry* (Brindley & Crocco, 2010).

Creating Equitable Classrooms Through Action Research shares the research of 10 educators from the Madison, Wisconsin, Metropolitan School District, all whose wonderings developed because of their passion to make their school district a more equitable place for all learners. *Taking Action With Teacher Research* shares the research of six teacher researchers from the Teacher Network Leadership Institute in New York, all whose wonderings developed as result of their passion to become politically active. *Empowering the Voice of the*

Teacher Researcher: Achieving Success Through a Culture of Inquiry shares the research of six teacher researchers from a single school in Florida, all whose wonderings developed because of their passion for middle school children. These are just a few examples of the many collections available as valuable resources to inspire wonderings.

In addition to the numerous published collections of teacher research, many professional organizations regularly publish teacher research in their journals and welcome teacher researchers as presenters at their state and national conferences. A few minutes searching the websites and journals of your favorite professional organization, such as NSTA (National Science Teachers Association), NCTM (National Council for Teachers of Mathematics), NCSS (National Council for the Social Studies), NCTE (National Council for Teachers of English), and NAEYC (National Association for the Education of Young Children), can lead you to many powerful publications by practitioners of their research. In turn, these practitioners' research can stimulate your wonderings.

Use the three general strategies just described—talking, brainstorming, and reading—to define your wondering. For additional direction, a number of specific exercises designed explicitly for the purposes of wondering development can be found in Chapter 2 of *The Reflective Educator's Guide to Classroom Research* (Dana & Yendol-Hoppey, 2009). Pause now to develop your wondering, and before continuing, write your wondering in the space here:

While you have now articulated a question to explore, it's important to realize the following:

> Rarely does any teacher researcher eloquently state his or her wondering immediately. It takes time, brainstorming, and actually 'playing' with the question . . . By playing with the wording of a wondering, teachers often fine-tune and discover more detail about the subject they are really passionate about understanding." (Dana & Yendol-Silva, 2009, pp. 57–58)

The purpose of the final section of this chapter is to help you "play" with your question by taking the wondering litmus test.

The Wondering Litmus Test

Chemists use a litmus test to determine if a substance is an acid or a base. You will use a litmus test to determine if the statement of your potential wondering for teacher inquiry is worthy of exploration and if it is articulated in such a way that exploration of the wondering will be the most valuable it can be for gaining insights into your teaching. The wondering litmus test consists of a series of questions that will help you reframe and refine your wondering until you have clearly and concisely articulated a question that generates excitement, enthusiasm, and intrigue.

Begin by copying the question you wrote in the previous section of this chapter onto a piece of scrap paper to keep by your side as you consider your wondering in relationship to each of the litmus test questions. You can use this scrap paper to tweak or even change your wondering as you progress through each question.

Question 1: Is your wondering something you are passionate about exploring?

Because the acts of teaching and learning are so complex, teachers know that their chosen profession is demanding work. Engaging in the act of teaching and simultaneously positioning oneself to study that act as you are in the midst of it can be a challenge. For that reason, it's important that teacher inquirers are passionate about what they choose to explore through the process of inquiry. Being passionate about your topic will provide you the energy needed to sustain your research over time.

As you have discovered through brainstorming, all teacher researchers have numerous possibilities for their research. One of the beauties of the inquiry process is it can help teachers focus their energies on one issue, tension, dilemma, or problem in their classroom rather than drown in the sea of possibilities for exploration. Yet for a laser-like focus to be maintained, it must be accompanied by a strong desire for learning about the topic at hand.

Working with your wondering until you are sure it is one you are passionate about exploring is perhaps the most important exercise you can engage in at the start of your inquiry. The importance of passion cannot be underestimated, and while it may seem like a simple thing to do, finding passion in a teaching dilemma is easier said than done. Unfortunately, because teachers are generally given limited opportunity to have a say in their professional development (Desimone, 2009), for years, professional development has been something done *to* teachers *by* others. When others define what we should learn over and over again for years, it isn't uncommon to forget what it can feel like to define your own learning and the excitement defining your own learning can bring!

Working on a wondering to find passion in a teaching dilemma is exemplified by Steve, a chemistry teacher I supported in the inquiry process. Steve was a member of a cross-disciplinary professional learning community at his high school that met on a regular basis to support one another's action research. At the start of his inquiry, Steve initially articulated a frustration with his students' performance on the tests he gave, and he wanted to develop a research question that would enable him to look at his assessment strategies and complete an item analysis of students' performance on these assessment measures.

Noticing as he spoke that Steve's body language and tone of voice was not exuding excitement about this possible direction for research, members of his PLC posed some questions to help Steve reflect on the direction of his wondering. By answering questions such as "What would you expect to learn about your students from this inquiry?" Steve began to realize that his real frustration didn't lie with students' performance on the tests themselves but with the extra-help sessions that prepared students for the tests. In recent months, some of Steve's students had begun goofing off in class and coming later for extra help, expecting Steve to reteach the same things he had done in class because they were not paying attention. At the same time, he had students coming in for extra help who were serious "A" students and wanted to deepen their understandings of chemistry with supplemental material as well as ensure their continued high performance on exams. Extra help time had become stressful for Steve in trying to meet the needs of these two very different types of students.

As Steve spoke about this with his PLC members, his facial expressions, voice tone, and body language were vibrant, and Steve realized the extra-help sessions were his real passion. The development of his wondering evolved from

- *In what ways can I make the chemistry exams I use to assess my students better?*

to

- *What is the most productive way to structure afterschool help sessions?*
- *What are students' perceptions and expectations for extra help?*
- *How does one create a student-driven versus teacher-driven afterschool session?*

With the help of his colleagues, Steve discovered a topic he was truly passionate about exploring.

Like Steve, now it's time for you to assess your stated wondering for the presence of passion. Before continuing with the litmus test, look carefully at your wondering. Did you chose a topic for exploration that you are truly passionate about exploring so you don't risk losing the commitment necessary to sustain your research overtime? If not, revisit the strategies for defining your wondering discussed in this chapter, and make a new selection that piques your curiosity and ignites your passion for teaching and the provision of powerful instruction for your students.

Question 2: Is your wondering focused on student learning?

The target goal for everything one does as a teacher is student learning. However, because the complexity of teaching springs forth many possibilities for exploration for every teacher inquirer, sometimes wonderings aren't directly related to student learning and may instead focus on such things as behavior management and time management. While things like behavior management and time management can certainly play a huge role in the classroom and are worthy topics for exploration through the process of inquiry, it's always important to be sure that the wondering you are posing in some way relates back to *student learning* so that, as teacher researchers, we never lose sight of our target goal when so many factors are competing for our attention in the classroom. After all, one of the coolest factors about practitioner research as a form of teacher professional development is that it wraps the learning of teachers around the learning of students!

Working on a wondering to ensure it is focused on student learning is exemplified by Pam, a first-grade teacher I supported in the inquiry process. At the time of her inquiry, Pam had been teaching for 25 years, and she had accumulated what she referred to as an amazing amount of teaching "stuff." Her classroom was cluttered and crowded, and she believed the clutter had gotten to a point that it was affecting both her and her students' outlook on the school day. In particular, her first graders' desks were arranged in tables, but they were so close together that students often bumped into each other when getting up from or returning to their desks. This sometimes led to student behavior problems that interfered with Pam's ability to circulate and assist individual learners as they engaged in individual and small group work.

Pam knew she was certainly passionate about cleaning up the clutter, reorganizing her classroom, and trying a new seating arrangement for her first-grade learners. Once she cleared out some teaching materials she no longer used, she thought it would be interesting to shift from having her students' desks arranged in table sets and instead try a horseshoe arrangement to create a better "flow of traffic" in her classroom as students moved to different stations, centers, and engaged in various activities in this lively first-grade classroom. She initially framed her wondering as "In what ways will arranging my first graders' desk in a horseshoe contribute to a better 'flow of traffic' as students come and go to their desks during the school day?"

While the organization of the space in which she did her teaching on a daily basis certainly is important and can contribute to creating a positive and healthy learning environment for young children, a closer examination of Pam's first wondering reveals that the wondering itself isn't directly related in any way to student learning. Through conversation with colleagues, Pam thought deeply about this issue and her attention was drawn to three special-needs students in her classroom who were easily distracted during individual and small-group time. These three learners struggled to complete assignments and engage in group work with their peers in meaningful ways. The more she thought about it, she wondered if these learners' distractibility would be decreased through her reorganization of the classroom as well as by teaching these three learners about organization and the ways being organized can contribute to their learning productivity in the classroom. She would use herself as a model as she targeted the organizational abilities of these three learners, cleaning out the classroom and reorganizing the desks. She would then use scaffolding with these three children in their own organizational plan to complete their individual work in a timely manner and make contributions to work done in groups.

The development of Pam's wondering evolved from

- *In what ways will arranging my first graders' desk in a horseshoe contribute to a better "flow of traffic" as students come and go to their desks during the school day?*

to

- *In what ways will implementing a minilesson series on organization with three first-grade special-needs students impact the quality of the work they are able to produce throughout the school day?*

With careful thought and reflection, Pam was able to keep her passion for cleaning out the clutter and rearranging students' desks as a part of her inquiry work, but she refined her wondering so that these actions would help her gain specific insights into the *learning* of her students.

Like Pam, now it's time for you to assess your stated wondering for a focus on student learning. Before continuing with the litmus test, look carefully at your wondering. Does your wondering relate to student learning in some meaningful way? If not, use the three strategies discussed in this chapter (talking, brainstorming, and reading) to develop ideas for directly connecting your original wondering to student learning. Refine your wondering accordingly.

Question 3: Is your wondering a real question (a question whose answer is not known)?

When teachers embark on practitioner inquiry for the first time, it is not uncommon to begin the inquiry journey in a comfortable place, for example, focusing attention on a pedagogical innovation that you have found success with in the past and have enthusiastically embraced already. Teachers often begin in their comfort zone because it feels safe and, perhaps, even empowering to have the opportunity to document some of the great teaching and learning that is occurring in the classroom. However, if you stay on this path, you risk investing time and energy into an inquiry that will merely confirm something you already know, and not lead to any new discoveries about your teaching.

Working on a wondering to make it real is exemplified by Lynn, a third-grade teacher I supported in the inquiry process. As a passionate advocate for technology and the meaningful integration of technology into teaching, it was no surprise that Lynn began her first inquiry with a focus on the latest technology gadget she had recently introduced into her classroom—the Interwrite pad. Lynn loved the fact that the Interwrite pad looked like a miniature whiteboard while interfacing with the computer, which allowed Lynn to teach from anywhere in the room. In addition, she found the use of the Interwrite pad highly motivated her students as they wrote on it and their writing was projected for the whole class to see during reading instruction. Exploding with enthusiasm for this new technology, Lynn articulated her first wondering as "How can I effectively use the Interwrite pad to teach reading?"

As she shared the background for this wondering with members of a PLC at her school, it was clear that Lynn had already introduced the writing pad into her reading instruction with exciting results. With some gentle probing from her colleagues, Lynn realized she already knew how to effectively use the Interwrite pad, but as she told the story of how motivating it had been for her students, she shared her observation that the struggling readers in her classroom did not respond in the same enthusiastic way as the rest of the class to this new technology. This part of Lynn's story provided an "aha moment" for Lynn about her initial wondering, leading her to consider multiple possibilities for shifts in her initial wondering from

- *How can I effectively use the Interwrite pad to teach reading in my third-grade classroom?*

to

- *How do I effectively teach struggling readers using the Interwrite pad?*

or

- *How do struggling third-grade readers experience the Interwrite pad?*

or

- *How do my struggling readers experience reading time in my third-grade classroom?*

By telling the story of her initial wondering development to her teaching colleagues, Lynn realized she already knew the answer to the question she had posed initially. Indeed, Lynn was already using the Interwrite pad quite effectively overall. The one exception to her successful use of the Interwrite pad was struggling readers, which seemed counterintuitive to Lynn. She believed the Interwrite pad would provide the perfect tactile experience for these struggling learners. What, possibly, could be going wrong? This question, which truly puzzled Lynn, became the impetus for her to explore various reworked possibilities for her initially stated wondering.

Like Lynn, now it's time for you to assess your stated wondering to be sure it is a real question. Before continuing with the litmus test, look carefully at your wondering. Is the wondering you selected something that deep down, you already know the answer to? If so, work to reframe or refocus your wondering in a more productive and valuable way.

Question 4: Is the wondering focused on your practice?

In addition to it being common for teachers to begin the inquiry process in their comfort zone, it is also common for teachers to initially focus their wondering on factors they may be frustrated about related to the teaching and learning context. When this happens, rather than being focused *inward* on one's teaching practice, a wondering might end up being focused *outward*, and initially framed around controlling or changing others (administrators, teaching colleagues, or even students themselves).

The problem with a wondering that is focused *outward* on changing the actions and behaviors of others is that the actions of others are outside of a teacher's control. An important premise of practitioner inquiry is that the only person a teacher can control is him- or herself. Wonderings that focus on changing the behavior of others rarely lead to the important self-discoveries about teaching that inquiry can reveal.

Working on a wondering to focus it on your own practice is exemplified by Jerry, a Spanish teacher I supported in the inquiry process. After many years successfully teaching foreign language in a brick and mortar context, Jerry took a job in a large virtual school to afford him more time and flexibility in his family life. While he estimated he actually worked more hours each week than he did in his old high school, he enjoyed being able to attend his children's school events without needing to take a personal day and create lessons plans for a sub. While he enjoyed virtual school teaching, at times, he became frustrated with students who didn't log into the course for weeks—How could he possibly teach students who didn't "show up" for weeks on end?

When his virtual school provided the option of engaging in inquiry to earn a substantial amount of professional development points teachers needed each year to remain employed, Jerry jumped at the opportunity to investigate his frustration and framed the question, "How do I get my Spanish II students who don't log into the course for two weeks or more to get their act together, catch up, and stay on pace?" He eagerly and enthusiastically shared his question with his administrator, an experienced virtual school teacher with a great deal of knowledge about action research.

With years of virtual school teaching under her belt, Jerry's administrator empathized with Jerry's dilemma, but knew that the way Jerry was framing his question wasn't likely to get him very far in his quest to help all of his students be successful and increase his course completion rate. Through discussion, Jerry's administrator helped him reframe his initial question from

- *How do I get my Spanish II students who don't log into the course for two weeks or more to get their act together, catch up, and stay on pace?*

to

- *What strategies can I incorporate as a virtual school teacher to support my Spanish II students who have fallen significantly behind the pacing schedule and/or have logged into the class infrequently?*

This wondering was accompanied by the following subquestions:

- *What are some reasons my students struggle to stay on pace?*
- *How do I support them without stressing them out?*

By discussing his wondering with an understanding administrator, Jerry was able to shift the focus of his wondering from *controlling* when, where, and how often his students logged into the class to *understanding* his students better and studying strategies he could employ to support them.

Like Jerry, now it's time for you to assess your stated wondering to be sure it focuses on your practice. Before continuing with the litmus test, look carefully at your wondering. Is your wondering focused on *controlling* or *changing the behavior* of others? If so, try reframing the wondering in a way that helps you *understand* (rather than control) others' behavior and allows you to discover what *you* can do as a teacher with those new understandings.

Question 5: Is your wondering phrased as a dichotomous (yes/no) question?

Recall that one of the major reasons we engage in teacher inquiry in the first place is because teaching and learning are such inherently complex activities. Practitioner inquires know that because teaching and learning are so complex, it's often counterproductive to pose a wondering that requires a simple yes/no answer. As inquirers, we are not after solely finding out if an intervention works. Teachers know that when working with students, conditions are so variable that an activity that works with one learner might not work with another in the same way, and a lesson that works one year or even in one class period might fall flat on its face the next.

Rather, as inquirers, we are interested in finding out how and why something is working or not working and even posing the question, "What does it mean for something to *work* in the first place?" Hence, to honor the great complexity inherent in teaching and learning, in general, teacher researchers do not phrase their wonderings as simple yes/no questions.

Working on a wondering to rephrase it from a simple yes/no question is exemplified by Karen, a reading coach I supported in the inquiry process. Karen was a student in my graduate class on practitioner research when she formulated her first wondering. At the time, in her work as a reading coach, she was interested in helping the teachers she coached better understand and use the new state assessment system designed to provide teachers screening, diagnostic, and progress monitoring information deemed by the state of Florida as essential to guiding instruction. It was part of her responsibility as the reading coach to help teachers use this system known as FAIR (Florida Assessments for Instruction in Reading). With a passion for helping teachers understand and effectively use this new system, she phrased her first wondering as

- *Does an analysis of FAIR (Florida Assessments for Instruction in Reading) data change teacher instructional practice?*

With some gentle probing from me as the instructor of the class, I helped her think about ways to rephrase her wondering in more open-ended terms, providing the following two possibilities for her consideration:

- *What is the relationship between teachers' analysis of FAIR data and changes they make to their reading practice?*

or

- *In what ways does teachers' analysis of FAIR data contribute to their professional growth and learning?*

Over the next few weeks, Karen continued to play with the wording of her wondering with her classmates to tweak it into a final form. She was careful to phrase the final wondering in an open-ended manner that invited many possibilities for the ways her research might unfold to capture the great complexity inherent in the work of a reading coach.

Like Karen, now it's time for you to assess your stated wondering to be sure it is phrased in an open-ended fashion. Before continuing with the litmus test, look carefully at your wondering. Is your wondering phrased as a simple yes/no question? If you have framed your initial question in dichotomous terms, try reframing it using one of the following phrases:

- *In what ways does . . .*
- *What is the relationship between . . .*
- *How do students experience . . .*
- *What happens when . . .*
- *How does . . .*

Question 6: Is your wondering specific?

While teacher researchers generally work to phrase their wonderings in an open-ended manner, they also work to make the wondering as specific as possible. Continuing to play with your wondering as the design of your study evolves and adding specific details to the framing of your wondering helps teacher researchers better communicate the detail of their studies to others. Three key components you might include in your wondering are the following:

- Participants (i.e., third-grade learners)
- Intervention/strategy/action
- Targeted skills/knowledge/ability outcomes

Working on a wondering to make it more specific is exemplified by Rachel, a third-grade teacher I supported in the inquiry process. Rachel engaged in inquiry as a part of her district's professional development program and originally set out to study this question:

- *What is the relationship between my students' participation in an online learning community and their learning?*

As Rachel worked with other teachers in her school to plan her inquiry, she began to tweak her wondering to make it more specific and ended up with the following:

- *In what ways will my third graders' participation in an online learning community effect their development as readers (as measured on the FAIR) as well as their motivation for learning?*

Through tweaking that initial wondering as her inquiry took shape, Rachel was able to name the participants (third-grade reading students), the action or intervention she tried as a teacher (participation in an online learning community), and the knowledge, skills, and abilities she wished to target (development as readers as measured on FAIR and student attitudes for learning).

As in Rachel's case, often these details are easier to include and work into your wondering as you think about other aspects of your study—your plan of action, how you will collect and analyze data, and a timeline for your inquiry to unfold. We'll be looking closely at these aspects of inquiry design in the next chapter. Keep the wondering you've defined and refined in Chapter 2 close at hand, and as you continue to flesh out other components of your inquiry in Chapter 3, consider returning to your wondering to make it more specific at this time.

3

Developing and Fine-Tuning Your Research Plan

Developing a plan for your inquiry requires careful thought about the ways you will collect data. I've learned that data are everywhere in my classroom. All creating an inquiry plan means for me is charting a course for how to capture it all. I particularly find student work and student interviews powerful data collection tools to help me not only gain insights into whatever my wondering is for a particular inquiry but to get to know my students in ways I never did before I inquired. There's not doubt that becoming an inquirer has made me a better teacher and has allowed me to better understand and reach each individual student in my classroom.

Mod 8

—Stephanie Whitaker, Teacher Inquirer,
Dunnedin Elementary School

The Research Plan Defined

A research plan is defined as an organizational structure for the ways the inquiry will be carried out. As a natural outgrowth of the research wondering that has been articulated and refined, the core feature of the research plan is an articulation of the ways the teacher researcher proposes to collect data. Data collection for the teacher researcher refers to the process of capturing the action and learning that is occurring in the classroom so it can be returned to by the teacher researcher at a later time. Capturing classroom action and learning as data allow the teacher researcher to systematically analyze and reflect on the outcomes of teaching and learning to create new insights and understandings in relationship to the research wondering. For the teacher researcher, the most prevalent form of data collection is usually *student work*, but there are many additional powerful ways that teacher researchers capture action and learning in their classrooms. These include the following:

- Field notes/anecdotal notes/running records
- Documents (such as lesson plans, curriculum guides, school policy, textbooks, Individual Educational Plans [IEPs], district memos, parent newsletters, progress reports, teacher plans books, and correspondence to and from parents, the principals, and specialists)
- Interviews (individual and group)
- Digital pictures
- Video
- Reflective journals
- Weblogs
- Surveys
- Quantitative measures of student achievement (standardized test scores, assessment measures including progress monitoring tools, and grades)
- Feedback from colleagues (often obtained through learning community or critical friend group work)
- Literature

More information and detail about each of the data collection-strategies named previously can be found in *The Reflective Educator's Guide to Classroom Research: Learning to Teach and Teaching to Learning Through Practitioner Research* (Dana & Yendol-Hoppey, 2009).

How to Define Your Research Plan

To define your research plan, begin by brainstorming a list of data collection strategies you might employ by creating a data collection chart. Title your chart with the wondering you developed and refined in Chapter 2. Next, generate two columns: (1) What information might help me answer my question? and (2) What data collection strategies would generate this information? Figure 3.1 provides an example of a Data Collection Brainstorm Chart. As you develop your chart, don't hold back—list *all* the possibilities in this brainstorming phase.

Once you have completed your chart, it is time to make some choices. Through developing your data collection brainstorm chart, you have compiled a comprehensive list of potential data collection strategies that could provide you with insights into your wondering. Consider each collection strategy on your list one by one.

- What would be the pros and cons of designing an inquiry that incorporated each of these data collection strategies?
- Which data collection strategies have the potential to provide the biggest insights into your wondering?

Figure 3.1   Data Collection Brainstorm Chart

Wondering: In what ways do science talks enhance student understandings of science concepts?	
Information That Would Help Me Answer My Question	*Data Collection Strategies That Would Generate This Information*
Knowing how students' conceptual knowledge during our astronomy unit develops	Collect the students' science journals
Knowing what students are saying during science talks	Audio taping science talks Taking field notes
My thinking about what happened during the science talks after they occur	Teacher journal
Students' opinions about science talks	Surveys
Literature on science talks; I'm already familiar with Karen Gallas's book *Talking Their Way Into Science*	Do a search for other books or articles that are connected to science talks, building conceptual knowledge in science, teaching elementary science, etc.

Source: Dana & Yendol-Hoppey (2009). *The Reflective Educator's Guide to Classroom Research: Learning to Teach and Teaching to Learn Through Practitioner Inquiry.* Thousand Oaks, CA: Corwin. Reprinted by permission.

Based on your answer to these questions, circle a few data collection strategies that you wish to carry forward into the design of your inquiry. Keep your data collection brainstorm chart by your side as you proceed with the next portion of this section.

With your data collection brainstorming completed, the next step in defining your research plan is to create an inquiry brief. An inquiry brief is a one- or two-page outline completed before your research study begins (Hubbard & Power, 1999). A research brief may cover such aspects as the purpose of your study, your wonderings, how you will collect data, what interventions/actions/new strategies you will try (any instructional plans related to the inquiry), how you will analyze data, and a detailed timeline for how your study will unfold. Three sample inquiry briefs appear at the end of this chapter (completed by a high school social studies teacher, a reading coach, and an ESL teacher, respectively). Using these briefs as a guide, pause now to create your inquiry brief, and return to this chapter once you have completed this task.

While you have now articulated a research plan, it's important to realize that rarely does a quality plan for research take shape immediately. It takes time, tweaking, and actually playing with changes and adjustments to your plan as you begin to develop the "big picture" of what your inquiry will look like. Hence, just as you did with your wondering, it is important to take some time to play with your plan. The purpose of the final section of this chapter is to help you do so by taking the inquiry plan litmus test.

The Inquiry Plan Litmus Test

Chemists use a litmus test to determine if a substance is an acid or a base. You will use a litmus test to determine if the plan you created for your inquiry is the best it can be to gain insights into the wondering you created and refined in Chapter 2. Similar to the wondering litmus test, the inquiry brief litmus test consists of a series of questions that will help you refine your plan for inquiry until you feel you have established the best possible route for your inquiry journey. Begin by printing the inquiry brief you created in the last section. You can edit your plan and make notes to yourself on this document as you progress through the litmus test.

Question 1: Do your data collection strategies align with your wondering and all other aspects of your inquiry plan?

When developing a plan for your inquiry, it's important that each piece of your inquiry is in alignment with the others. For example, if the dilemma that led to your wondering was the quest to increase one of your learning disabled student's multiplication fact fluency while simultaneously helping that student develop conceptual understanding of multiplication, you wouldn't do activities with the student focused on fractions and decimals, and you wouldn't incorporate a progress monitoring tool designed to trace reading fluency. While this might seem like an outlandish example, it can be challenging to select data collection strategies that tightly align with your wondering and your plan for action because teaching and learning are such complicated endeavors and there are so many questions we could explore, actions we can try, and potential data sources we could invoke to understand our actions and the impact we are having on student learning.

Putting together your plan for inquiry is like the old children's song "I Know an Old Lady," written by Rose Bonne and Alan Mills. In this song, one fascinating swallowing of an object leads logically and sequentially to the next, building throughout the song to the swallowing of a cow:

> She swallowed the cow to catch the goat . . .
>
> She swallowed the goat to catch the dog . . .
>
> She swallowed the dog to catch the cat . . .
>
> She swallowed the cat to catch the bird . . .
>
> She swallowed the bird to catch the spider
>
> That wiggled and wiggled and tickled inside her.
>
> She swallowed the spider to catch the fly.
>
> But I don't know why she swallowed that fly,
>
> Perhaps she'll die.

Your inquiry should be designed to work just like the old lady, swallowing away in a planned, intentional, systematic, and connected way. Your background dilemma, wondering, data collection, and analysis strategies should all flow logically from each individual component of your inquiry plan to the next.

- The strategies you are invoking to collect data should make perfect sense in relationship to the statement of your wondering.
- Your wondering should flow naturally and logically from your description of an issue, tension, problem, or dilemma in your teaching practice that led to your inquiry.
- Your selection of a teaching action, intervention, or strategy that you might try should make perfect sense in relationship to your articulated dilemma and wondering.
- The data you collect and analyze should emerge naturally from the action/intervention/strategy you employ.

Now it's time for you to assess your inquiry plan for alignment. Before continuing with the litmus test, look carefully at your brief. Do all the components of your inquiry align with one another? If not, adjust and tweak individual components of your inquiry until each component aligns with the next.

Question 2: Are you using multiple forms of data to gain insights into your wondering?

Throughout the litmus test questions about wondering development and inquiry plan design so far, we've been reminded repeatedly about the complexity inherent in the acts of teaching and learning as a primary reason engagement in inquiry is such an important part of teaching in the first place! Teacher researchers inquire because they want to untangle some of that great complexity inherent in their daily work and engage in a continuous cycle of improvement, truly becoming the best teachers they can be!

As teacher researchers work to untangle the complexities of teaching, they know that any one data source, no matter what that data source is and how much stock others put into that data source (such as scores on a standardized test or observational notes that a teacher takes as she carefully observes a student at work), can only provide a limited perspective on the acts of teaching and learning. Hence, most teacher researchers choose to use more than one source of data to gain insights into their wonderings, with perhaps one of the most prevalent data sources simply being student work.

Now, it's time for you to assess your inquiry plan for data sources. Before continuing with the litmus test, look carefully at your brief.

Have you incorporated more than one data collection strategy into your inquiry plan? If not, return to the listing of data collection strategies that appear in the opening section of this chapter and/or your data collection brainstorm chart for some additional data collection ideas and incorporate these into your inquiry plan.

Question 3: Does one of the forms of data you will collect include literature and/or have you already used literature to frame your wondering?

Although we often do not think of literature as data, literature offers an opportunity to think about how your work as a teacher inquirer is informed by, and connected to, the work of others. No one teaches or inquires in a vacuum. When we engage in the act of teaching, we are situated within a context (our particular classroom, grade level, school, district, state, country, etc.), and our context mediates much of what we do and understand as teachers. Similarly when teachers inquire, their work is situated within a large, rich, preexisting knowledge base that is captured in such things as books, journal articles, newspaper articles, conference papers, and websites. Looking at this preexisting knowledge base on teaching informs your study. "Literature is an essential form of data that every teacher-inquirer should use so as to be connected to, informed by, and a contributor to the larger conversation about educational practice" (Dana & Yendol-Hoppey, 2009, p. 112).

It is important to note that when conceptualizing literature as one data source to inform your research and practice, you should use the literature rather than letting the literature use you! Teacher researchers let the literature "use" them when they think in terms of developing a traditional exhaustive review of the literature in the same ways academics do when they are writing for publication in referred research journals or as graduate students do when they are writing a dissertation or thesis. While thorough reviews of literature are important for these constituencies as they generate theory and knowledge on a large scale and may be a part of the practitioner inquiry process when undertaken as a part of graduate work at a university, this conceptualization of literature use is not consonant with the daily local work of classroom teachers who may not have access to a university library and do not have the time to spend days and weeks researching and reading articles related to their topic of study when they are simultaneously engaging in the act of teaching every day.

Using the literature, rather than letting the literature use you, simply means selecting *some* reputable works from the preexisting knowledge base on teaching that connect to your wonderings and will give you insights as your study is unfolding. Teacher inquirers generally collect literature at two different times: (1) when they first define or are in the process of defining a wondering (as previously discussed in Chapter 2) and (2) as their studies lead them to new findings and new wonderings. In these cases, teachers use the literature to become well informed on what current knowledge exists in the field related to their topic.

When engaging in the act of inquiry, teacher researchers "treat both their own practice as the site for intentional investigation and the knowledge and theory produced by others as generative material for interrogation and interpretation" (Cochran-Smith & Lytle, 2009, p. 131). Hence, to *use* the literature means critically analyzing what has been written and published related to your topic of study and drawing relationships between the knowledge and the theory produced by others and the knowledge you are generating locally from practice.

Now, it's time for you to assess your inquiry plan for the incorporation of literature. Before continuing with the litmus test, look carefully at your brief. Have you incorporated the exploration of literature into your plan? If not, use a search engine such as Google Scholar to find research related to your study and/or ask other teachers and support personnel in your district (such as the math coach, reading coach, professional development director, etc.) for recommendations of literature that connects to your inquiry topic and might inform your work.

Question 4: Is the design of your study experimental?

When teachers hear the word *research*, one image that is often conjured in their minds is that of a scientist in a lab coat working with lab rats, formulating hypotheses, and setting up comparison groups— one to receive a "treatment" and one to remain "the control." Because the word *research* carries so much baggage with it, it is not uncommon for first-time teacher researchers to be drawn to traditional experimental study designs in the early stages of developing a plan for their research, assigning a child or group of children to continue business as usual in the classroom (serving as a control group) and a child or group of children to engage with the teacher in a new program, intervention, or activity that is the subject of study.

Yet rarely does it make sense for an action research study to take an experimental form, as teacher action research is generally about capturing the natural actions that occur in the busy, real world of the classroom. In addition, by and large, a single teacher's classroom usually is not a ripe place to design an experimental study since the sample size used in the study generally would not be adequate to indicate any statistical differences, and any one treatment variable would almost be impossible to isolate from intervening variables. Finally, one would need to question the ethics of providing a potentially beneficial "treatment" to some children within a classroom but not to all.

Example: A Fourth-Grade Teacher Recasts Her Initial Experimental Research Design

The original conceptualization of a study as experimental is exemplified by Debbi, a fourth-grade teacher I coached in the inquiry process. Debbi was passionate about reading and, in particular, fluency. Debbi's school had been 1 of 13 schools to pilot a statewide program called the Florida Reading Initiative. In addition, her school had set a goal as part of their annual school improvement planning process to raise the fluency levels of their lowest achieving students to increase their performance on the reading portion of their state's standardized test—FCAT (Florida Comprehensive Achievement Test). Finally, Debbi was a voracious reader and had been studying the literature on reading fluency. She knew the research indicated that there is a correlation between fluency and comprehension.

With the knowledge that research indicated repeated readings improve fluency, Debbi began the design of her inquiry seeking to find if there would be a difference in fluency gains between using a commercial reading program her district had purchased called Great Leaps and repeated readings of plays with her students. In particular, Debbi owned a book of "fractured fairy tale plays," humorous takes on traditional fairy tales, that Debbi believed would be very motivational for fourth-grade learners, and more likely than the commercial reading program to elicit a joy of reading in her struggling readers. Debbi proceeded to conceptualize an inquiry that entailed dividing her lowest performing students into two different reading groups— using the Great Leaps Program with one group and the fractured fairy tales with the other group. She indicated in her inquiry brief that she planned to compare both groups' scores using a progress monitoring tool designed to measure reading fluency to see which group had higher gains.

In coaching Debbi in the design of her inquiry, I first provided some warm, supportive feedback, but then suggested she might simplify her inquiry a bit and posed the question, "If you weren't about to embark on an action research project, would you, in the natural ways that you think about teaching, assign your struggling readers to two different groups and teach them in two different ways?"

Debbi responded that she would not. Rather, she would just try the use of fractured fairy tales with all of her struggling readers and see what kinds of results she might get.

"Okay then," I replied. "If you wouldn't assign kids to two differently taught groups as a natural part of your teaching, then you might want to rethink your initial plan for inquiry. Would it work for you if you developed a plan to try fractured fairy tales with all of your struggling readers and look closely at the ways the introduction of this new strategy plays out in the classroom? In essence, rather than looking at cause and effect, you would be looking at the general relationship that develops between the reading of fractured fairy tales and fluency development in struggling fourth-grade learners over time."

Debbi agreed that this plan felt more comfortable to her and that she could still use the fluency progress monitoring measure as an indicator of fluency growth for data. She brainstormed other forms of data that also might provide insights into her students' experiences with fractured fairy tale plays. She decided to take observational notes as her students read these plays, collect all work that was generated by the students that related to her reading instruction with fractured fairy tales, as well as have her students compose "Dear Mrs. Hubbell" letters where they would tell her what they liked and disliked about reading fractured fairy tales. With this new plan, she adjusted her inquiry brief accordingly.

Like Debbi, now it's time for you to assess your inquiry plan. Before continuing with the litmus test, look carefully at your brief. Is your study designed with a "comparison" and "control" group? If so, try reframing the study design to capture natural actions that are occurring in the busy real world of your classroom.

Question 5: Is the inquiry plan doable?

The inquiry process is definitely one that causes energy and excitement for many teachers when they are given the opportunity to take charge of their professional learning, sometimes for the first time in their careers! This energy and excitement can sometimes lead to inquiry overboard syndrome. Inquiry overboard syndrome occurs when a teacher gets so caught up in the possibilities when planning research that the inquiry plan ends up resembling a complex longitudinal research study that would take years to implement and/or would require writing an entire book or even several volumes of a book about the research undertaking to do the inquiry justice!

Teacher researchers know that a certain amount of realism is an important ingredient to planning an inquiry. Furthermore, practitioner researchers have the potential to make real and lasting impact on classroom practice only when engagement in inquiry becomes a part of teaching practice, rather than exist apart from it. Hence, a plan for inquiry must be doable and include the collection of *reasonable* amounts and *reasonable* types of data. Whenever possible, data collection strategies should emerge from what is a natural part of the teaching act already (such as the generation of student work).

The danger of creating an inquiry plan that is too ambitious or overboard is that when the realization of the magnitude of the plan hits the teacher researcher while she is in the midst of doing the research, she is more likely to abandon the process altogether than to adjust her expectations for the research midstream. Furthermore, she is more likely to conceptualize teaching and research as two separate entities, and not feel the dynamic interplay between the two. Marilyn Cochran-Smith and Susan Lytle (2009) call this important interplay "working the dialectic":

> The term *dialectic* refers to the tensions and presumed contradictions between a number of key ideas and issues that have to do with research, practice, and knowledge. The first, and perhaps most important of these, is the assumed dichotomy between research and practice; the second is the twin of the first—the assumed disjuncture between the role of the researcher and the role of the practitioner. When research and practice are assumed to be dichotomous, then analysis, inquiry, and theorizing are understood to be part and parcel of the world of research, while action, experience, and doing are considered integral to the world of practice.
>
> In contrast, practitioner research is defined, at least in part, by turning these dichotomies on their heads. With practitioner research, the borders between inquiry and practice are crossed, and the boundaries between being a researcher and being a practitioner are blurred. Instead of being regarded as oppositional constructs, then inquiry and practice are assumed to be

related to each other in terms of productive and generative tensions. From this perspective, inquiry and practice are understood to have a reciprocal, recursive, and symbiotic relationship, and it is assumed that it is not only possible, but indeed beneficial, to take on simultaneously the roles of both researcher and practitioner. This means that when school-based educators "work the dialectic" of inquiry and practice, there are not distinct moments when they are only researchers or only practitioner. Rather, these activities and roles are integrated and dynamic. (pp. 93–95)

Now it's time for you to assess your inquiry plan for doability. Before continuing with the litmus test, look carefully at your brief. Does what you are planning to do seamlessly integrate your role as teacher and your role as researcher so your inquiry plan meshes naturally with your daily practice? Is what you are planning to do reasonable to accomplish given all of the many responsibilities that are already a part of your teaching workday? If not, work to downsize your inquiry and limit your inquiry goals and aspirations to something that is reasonable to accomplish, yet meaningful to your practice and to your students' learning. Remember, inquiry is a cycle—you don't have to do everything in one pass through the cycle!

Question 6: Have you considered the possibilities of detours to your inquiry plan and built into your plan the flexibility necessary to take detours, if necessary, along the way?

Keep in mind that although you have used the first five inquiry brief litmus test questions to fine-tune the roadmap for your study, it is common for unexpected happenings to occur as you engage in the process of inquiry that may require you to take a detour from your plan. While you really can't plan for the unexpected, teacher researchers know that it is perfectly natural and normal to make shifts in plans as an inquiry unfolds. Rarely does any teacher inquirer articulate a perfect plan on paper that is tightly constructed and plays out exactly as originally planned.

The value of the inquiry brief is not to create a perfectly articulated document that will play out exactly as planned, but to get something down on paper to get you started on the next leg of your inquiry journey. As you begin to collect data and learn something that might shift the course of your journey, shift away! Have the courage to take detours in your plan if what you are learning from your data indicates that it is desirable and necessary to do so. Just keep track of changes you make to your plan along the way, as these changes become a valuable part of your learning journey and are important to share with others as a part of your inquiry story.

Gary Boulware

Purpose

As a new high school educator, I was interested in preparing students for college—especially first-generation college students. I noticed that the demographics of my AP students were overwhelmingly white and these students were the product of college-educated parents. After asking some questions, I discovered the school policy, which acted as a filter to signing up for AP classes: Student academic achievements as measured by the FCAT and GPA were the primary requirements for entry into the program. These filters were probably a good statistical indicator of a student's potential to have the work ethic and academics skills to be successful in an AP environment and to pass a rigorous AP exam. However, I wanted more nontraditional AP students to sign up and try an AP class. I wanted students who were previously excluded from being in AP classes afforded the experience of being in an academically rigorous classroom with focused traditional AP students. I believed I could raise the academic expectations of nontraditional AP students without slowing the pace of the class required to complete the AP curriculum.

To entice nontraditional AP students to enroll in AP classes and to provide for the very real possibility of formal assessment failure (such as AP-level unit tests and end of course exam), I decided to offer a "guaranteed C" to all students. The criteria for a guaranteed C was advertised as the following:

- If you attend class regularly,
- if you are not a pain in my backside,
- if you earn a minimum of 70% on every notebook check,
- if you take every test/quiz,
- if you complete points makeup after every test,

you will earn at least a C in my classes.

The intent was to provide a safety net for students new to the rigors of an AP environment and take some of the risk out of taking an AP course. I deeply believe that the success of this generation of future leaders and economic engine of our country depends on setting high expectations for students while they are still in high school. These standards will hopefully help them at the university level as well as throughout their lives. Existing research generally supports the notion that students who have the opportunity to take AP courses do better in college. The next section summarizes this research.

Background Research

There are a number of studies that indicate students who participate in an AP program derive benefits. In the article *The Relationship Between Advanced Placement and College Graduation,* Dougherty, Mellor, and Jian (2006) found a strong relationship between AP participation and college graduation rates. A similar conclusion may be found in *College Outcomes Comparisons by AP and Non-AP High School Experiences,* by Hargrove, Godin, and Dodd (2008). Research discussed in *Expanding Opportunity in Higher Education: Leveraging Promise* by Patricia C. Gándara, Gary Orfield, and Catherine L. Horn found that university admissions consider student completion of AP courses in admissions' processes.

This relationship, however, may be more complicated as discussed in *The Link Between Advanced Placement Experience and Early College Success.* In this article by Klopfenstien and Thomas (2006), the authors found that the basis for the strong relationship between taking AP courses and success in college might be more attributable to the "self-selection" nature of the type of students who take AP courses versus the impact of the AP curriculum itself and college success. In other words, the real independent variable is self-selection versus the impact of taking AP classes. In the article *Raising the Bar: Curricular Intensity and Academic Performance,* authors Attewell and Domina (2008) arrived at the following conclusion:

> Inequalities in curricular intensity are primarily explained by student socioeconomic status. . . . [There are] significant positive effects of taking a more intense curriculum on 12th-grade test scores and in probabilities of entry to and completion of college. However, the effect sizes of curricular intensity are generally modest. (p. 53)

Question

What are the implications for my students in offering a guaranteed C for completing assigned work, regardless of quiz and test performance in the AP classes I teach?

Method

This research involved collecting survey data to try to determine intended and unintended consequences of this practice. I will ask all of my AP students to take the survey and include open-ended questions on the survey as well. Next, I will interview different groups of students based on themes I see emerging after I analyze survey data. Finally, I will engage my teaching colleagues in discussion about the policy and what they have heard from students about this policy.

Calendar

Early October—Create survey—get feedback on survey from my learning community.

November—Administer survey to students.

Late November—Analyze survey results. Create charts and graphs to better understand my students' perspectives.

After Holiday Break (Jan)—Interview students based on what I learn from my survey.

February—Talk with teaching colleagues—Take notes on their perspectives on the guaranteed C policy.

March—Engage in data analysis meeting with learning community.

April—Present my research at P. K. Yonge's Inquiry and Investigations Luncheon.

References

Attewell, P., & Thurston D. (2008). Raising the bar: Curricular intensity and academic performance. *Educational Evaluation & Policy Analysis, 30*(1), 51–71.

Dougherty, C., Mellor, L., & Jian, S. (2006). *The relationship between advanced placement and college graduation.* (National Center for Educational Accountability: 2005 AP Study Series, Report 1). Austin, Texas: National Center for Educational Accountability.

Gándara, P. C., Orfield, G., & Horn, C. L. (2006). *Expanding opportunity in higher education: Leveraging promise.* Albany: State University of New York Press.

Hargrove, L., Godin, D., & Dodd, B. (2008). *College outcomes comparisons by AP and Non-AP high school experiences* Report NO. 2008-3. New York, NY: The College Board.

Klopfenstein, K., & Thomas, M. K. (2006). *The link between Advanced Placement experience and early college success.* Retrieved from http://www.utdallas.edu/research/tsp/pdfpapers/ap_coll.060706.pdf

Sample Inquiry Brief

Kathy Christensen

Purpose

As a summer school reading coach, I became acquainted with a struggling student who was often referred to me for discipline issues and noncompliant behavior. He is a Fresh Start student who is now in a sixth-grade intensive reading class. Unfortunately, many of his antisocial and alienating behaviors have continued. After reading *Creating Equitable Classrooms Through Action Research,* (Caro-Bruce, Flessner, Klehr, & Zeichner, 2007, in particularly Chapter 7), I began to ruminate about the possible use of service learning to enhance academic achievement and to examine its effects on a particular student's interpersonal skills. Research on service-learning appears to have a variety of learning goals and focus. Generally, elementary schools have schoolwide or gradewide service-learning programs, while middle and high schools are more likely to employ individual classes in service learning. Fostering civic responsibility and meeting community needs are often stated as reasons for using service-learning projects. Many states have service-learning student goals and many mandate service-learning hours for graduation.

In an article in *Phi Delta Kappan* (2000), Shelley Billig shared research on definitions of service-learning; evidence of impact; impact of service-learning on personal, social, and academic growth; and summarized key components of effective projects. Of particular interest to me were the following:

- Students who engaged in service-learning were more likely to treat one another kindly, help one another, and care about doing their best.
- Male middle-schoolers reported increased self-esteem and had fewer behavioral problems after engaging in service-learning.
- Students in service-learning programs in elementary and middle schools showed reduced levels of alienation and behavioral problems.
- Service-learning has a positive effect on students' interpersonal development and the ability to relate to culturally diverse groups.

According to the Wisconsin Department of Public Instruction guide, *High Quality Instruction That Transforms: A Guide to Implementing Quality Academic Service-Learning* (Evers, 2010), the service-learning process includes ongoing reflection and is linked to curriculum. An interesting outcome shared from the National Educational Longitudinal Study of 1988 (NELS) was that students who participated in service-learning scored 6.7% higher in reading achievement and 5.9% higher in science achievement than those who did not participate in service-learning.

Additionally, a study from New England schools (Klute, 2002) showed that sixth-grade service-learning participants in New Hampshire demonstrated statistically significant gains in achievement scores on state assessments relative to their performance in the past.

My wondering began around one challenging sixth-grade male student. Now I'm considering using a small group of sixth-grade students in the project. I'm wondering if the service-learning could be based on a school community need. Almost every year there is a drop in reading comprehension in second grade as compared to first-grade FAIR and SAT 10 scores. We have been working to increase comprehension strategy learning in the second-grade Core instructional time. I am wondering how the additional instructional support of upper-grade students might impact the second graders and meet their need of additional strategy practice.

Wondering

What is the relationship between implementing a buddy reading partnership program between sixth-grade and second-grade students and these students' social and academic growth?

Subwonderings

- Which comprehension strategies will be the most beneficial for each group of learners?
- How will the students' attitudes and confidence change because of this work?
- What will be the effects on the students' behavior regarding classroom behavior and referrals?

Method

I will meet with the sixth-grade students at the beginning of the week to discuss the comprehension strategy they will be teaching that week. We will identify key terms/language stems they can use when working with their second-grade reading buddies. For two more 30-minute sessions, the sixth graders will work with their second-grade buddies around the second graders' books of choice. During the 30-minute sessions, the sixth-grade buddies will model the strategy aloud and help their younger reading partner employ the strategy. The sixth graders will assess how their buddy is doing through observation and questioning. We will debrief and decide when it is time to move on to another strategy. I am hoping we can get through three comprehension strategies in the six weeks of the inquiry. The sixth graders will decide as a group which strategies we will use. We will work together in my classroom.

Data Collection

I will use pre- and post-learning strengths surveys with the sixth graders. I will also take field notes as I observe the pairs working together. Students' reading grades and weekly behavioral reports will also be analyzed. I will also ask the sixth graders to briefly reflect and assess each day's work in a minijournal. I will interview both groups of students at the end of the inquiry, as well as their classroom teachers.

Calendar

Oct. 7, 2010—Teachers select students. I will administer the self-strengths inventory to the sixth graders and introduce the inquiry project.

Week of Oct. 11th—Meet with sixth graders to select the first strategy, discuss, and plan. Introduce pairs and begin work, meeting three times this week.

Week of Oct. 18th—Meet three times this week.

Week of Oct. 25th—Meet three times this week, employing a new comprehension strategy.

Week of Nov. 1st—Meet three times this week.

Week of Nov. 8th—Meet three times this week, employing a new comprehension strategy.

Week of Nov. 15th—Meet three times this week.

Week of Nov. 22nd—Debrief with both groups, post-assess sixth graders, and begin data analysis.

References

Billig, S. (2000). Research on K–12 school-based service-learning: The evidence builds. *Phi Delta Kappan, 81,* 658–664.

Caro-Bruce, C., Flessner, R., Klehr, M., & Zeichner, K. M. (2007). *Creating equitable classrooms through action research.* Thousand Oaks, CA: Corwin.

Evers, T. (2010). *High quality instruction that transforms: A guide to implementing quality academic service-learning.* Madison: Wisconsin Department of Public Instruction. Retrieved from, http://dpi.wi.gov/fscp/slhmpage.html

Klute, M. M. (2002, December). *Antioch's community-based school environmental education (CO-SEED): Quantitative evaluation report.* Denver, CO: RMC Research Corporation.

Sample Inquiry Brief

Sharon Earle

Purpose

As an ESOL teacher, I work with ELLs of varying language proficiencies in Grades K–5. An area I have long recognized a personal need to develop further in my practice is in the development of language goals concurrent with content goals for reading specifically and language arts generally. My hope is that through researching and developing my practice in forming language objectives as part of planning, I will recognize more specificity related to language development in my teaching, I will recognize and be able to more effectively document ongoing language development/growth in my students, and the quality of the dialogue within my coteaching relationships related to language development around both ELLs and other students' language needs will increase in terms of analysis and for planning.

Background Research

Literacy development across content areas is a challenge for ELLs in mainstream classrooms. Key to supporting content learning, explicit academic language instruction should be a part of every lesson for minority-language students. NCLB requires that both language development and academic achievement be monitored annually. The reality, however, is that few teachers plan for and explicitly teach language through content area instruction.

CALLA (Cognitive Academic Language Learning Approach) and the Sheltered Instruction Observation Protocol, as well as Classroom Instruction that works with English Language Learners (Hill & Flynn, 2006) each argue the importance of content-based English language instruction in order to support language development while supporting ongoing academic development rather than allowing students to fall behind academically while gaining proficiency in the language.

The process of determining what language functions and structures to include as language objectives alongside content objectives is challenging, however. And though many teachers are aware of the need to document the use of strategies for making content learning comprehensible, they are not as aware of the importance of developing and explicitly teaching clear language goals.

Question

How will researching, developing, and implementing the practice of including language objectives for reading/language arts instruction affect my ability to recognize and document ongoing language development (as opposed to reading development alone) in my students and the analysis and planning of language instruction within my coteaching relationships?

Subquestions

- In what ways will modeling the practice of including language objectives with content objectives within the reading block affect planning in other content areas for the classroom teacher?
- How will explicit language development accelerate/affect the oral and written language development of ELLs?

Method

I coteach in a first-grade classroom and a third-grade classroom for part of the 90-minute reading block. In the first-grade coteaching environment, I coteach the word work routine, the minilesson for reading, and the teacher and I work together for conferring during independent reading and differentiated reading instruction through small-group guided reading. I am scheduled for an hour and 20 minutes of the first-grade reading block each day. In the third-grade classroom, I am scheduled for an hour and 15 minutes each day during which I support the vocabulary instruction, the minilesson and then confer with students during independent reading and provide small-group instruction. In implementing my inquiry, I plan to seek out resources that I hope will guide me in recognizing opportunities for explicit instruction around language development related to content objectives and that I will be able to discern the difference between language objectives and content objectives specific to a content area that is heavily language based to begin with. To clarify, it is sometimes difficult to separate language objectives from reading or language arts objectives as opposed to language objectives from science, social studies, or math objectives. As I begin to plan for language objectives, I will make them a part of my lesson introductions and wrap-ups to make the objectives explicit to both students and my coteaching partners. Prior to implementation of this teaching practice, I plan to interview the teachers with whom I coteach to learn more about their understanding of language development and planning for it. I also plan to assess oral language development of my first-grade ELL students and a few non-ELL students who may benefit from explicit language teaching as well as my third-grade ELL students for the purpose of gathering data to inform my instruction and to monitor language development, which will assist in planning dialogue between the teachers I coteach with and me. Along the way, my plan is to journal for the purpose of reflecting on my growth in practice as it relates to planning for language instruction as well as its effect on my students' language development and my coteaching efficacy for language instruction for ELLs.

Data Collection

- Field notes of personal journal reflections and teacher interviews
- Oral language pre- and post-assessments using levels sentences and diagnostic sentences—Record of Oral Language and Biks & Gutches (Clay, Gill, Glynn, McNaughton, & Salmon, 1999)
- Anecdotal records of student–teacher conversations related to language proficiency and developmental needs
- Lesson plans
- Documentation of student writing

Calendar

Weeks of Oct. 4–17

- Research resources for developing language objectives tied to content objectives
- Develop and refine inquiry brief
- Develop interview questions for teachers
- Begin reflective journal with a goal of a minimum of three entries per week

Week of Oct. 18–24

- Administer oral language assessment to first- and third-grade students
- Begin including language objectives as part of reading workshop objectives
- Begin including the development of language objectives as part of the planning process with teachers
- Continue reflective journaling
- Collect anecdotal records of language production from students

Weeks of Oct. 25–31 and Nov. 1–21

- Continue including language objectives as part of reading workshop objectives
- Continue including the development of language objectives as part of the planning process with teachers
- Continue reflective journaling
- Continue collecting anecdotal records of language production from students

Week of Nov. 15–21

- Interview teachers for post-study feedback
- Finish data collection of anecdotal records
- Administer oral language assessment to first- and third-grade students

Week of Nov. 22–28

- Begin data analysis
- Begin inquiry summary

References

Clay, M. M., Gill, M., Glynn, T., McNaughton, T., & Salmon, K. (2007). *Record of oral language: observing changes in the acquisition of language structures.* North Shore, New Zealand: Pearson.

Hill, J. D., & Flynn, K. M. (2006). *Classroom instruction that works with English language learners.* Alexandria, VA: Association of Supervision and Curriculum Development.

4

Analyzing Your Data

*When I was first confronted with data analysis, I was over-
whelmed. I felt "unqualified" to be a researcher. . . . But when I
forced myself to sit down with my data, it was as if I had turned
the wheel of a kaleidoscope and the picture I thought I was looking at changed. I realized I was seeing patterns in my data that
without looking closely, I would have missed. That's the thing
about being a teacher inquirer; it forces you to step back from the
myriad of happenings in your classroom, look closely at a particular wondering and find that your thoughtful analysis helps
you understand something deeply.*

—Marisa Ramirez Stukey, Teacher Inquirer,
P. K. Yonge Developmental Research School

Data Analysis Defined

Data analysis is an ongoing and critical component of the teacher
inquiry experience, and can be defined simply as developing an
understanding of what your data are telling you based on a close,
careful, and critical examination of them overtime and subsequently,
creating a story of your learning as an inquirer that is data rich. A
data-rich story of professional learning is carefully crafted to provide sufficient evidence to warrant the claims you wish to make

from your study as well as the actions you plan to take in your practice as a result of your investigation.

The process of data analysis is twofold: formative and summative.

Formative Data Analysis

Formative data analysis takes place throughout the inquiry study. The processes of data collection and data analysis do not exist independently of one another and proceed in a chronological lockstep manner. Rather, these processes are iterative in nature. As teacher researchers collect data throughout a study, they seek to understand what those data mean and use these understandings to make decisions about instruction and the next steps in their inquiry journey.

Example: A Seventh-Grade Science Teacher Analyzes Data at the Start of Her Inquiry

Formative data analysis is exemplified by May, a middle school teacher I supported in the inquiry process along with her inquiry coach, Darby Delane. In line with the National Science Standards, May was dedicated to investigation-based science teaching, where her students would actually experience the scientific process as much as possible, like real scientists. May liked to design her lessons to be action oriented, having students spend a majority of their time engaged in activities, such as, "asking questions, mixing chemicals, dissecting flowers, observing ants, and forming hypotheses before trying them out" (Wolk, 2008, p. 118). Yet after a two-week break in the teaching routine because of testing and spring break, students were not behaving in ways conducive to May's implementation of an investigation-based curriculum and a positive classroom-learning environment. May found herself retreating from her investigation-based teaching methods and turned to direct, lecture-based instruction in an effort to "control" her students. Through discussions with her seventh-grade team, May realized she missed her investigation-based teaching methods and lamented that she was no longer able to teach science in ways that were consonant with her philosophy and best teaching practices advocated by the National Science Teachers Association. May realized that to return to investigation-based work at the end of the school year with her students, she needed to take a step back in order to take a step forward, looking closely at her classroom management. And so May turned to teacher research and embarked on her first cycle of the inquiry process by wondering, "How can I create the classroom management conditions needed so my students can be successful science learners?" (Delane, Dana, & Steward, 2010)

The inquiry plan she constructed called for the initial collection of data through leading a whole-class focus group interview with her fourth-period students to involve them in envisioning what a classroom environment conducive to learning science would look like. She began class by sharing with the students her observations of their behavior since coming back from two weeks of state testing and spring break, noting that because of their behavior, she had retreated from teaching science in the ways they all enjoy. She posed this whole-class focus group interview question to the class, "How we can work together to create the classroom conditions needed so we can all learn science in interesting ways?"

Students offered their ideas, while May recorded them on a large piece of chart paper at the front of the room. As May was recording responses, she noticed that only a handful of her entire class of students was participating. She remembered reading in *The Reflective Educator's Guide to Research* that one of the limitations of focus group interviews was that "less confident focus-group members refrain from sharing their thoughts" (Dana & Yendol-Hoppey, 2009, p. 85). With this in mind, May told her students they were going to end their discussion with each class member writing one wish for their class so that at the end of the year, they would all feel that they were successful science learners. May thought that by collecting written responses, every student's "voice" would be heard.

To analyze these responses, that evening on her computer, May typed the 21 wishes that were turned in. After reading through all responses a few times, May experimented with grouping these responses in various ways. For example, she sorted the responses by gender. She took careful note of the responses made by her most struggling students. Finally, she settled on grouping the responses into three different categories, and highlighted each category:

Category 1 (7 responses): Wishes for more fun and less pressure
from school

Category 2 (5 responses): Wishes for a more calm and respectful
environment

Category 3 (9 responses): Wishes for more consistency in class
routine

Student Wish List Responses

1. Give respect to Ms. Steward and other classmates. Let's be kind and no arguing with one another.

2. I wish everyone would get an A and that we had more field trips.

3. Have our agenda done when Ms. Steward comes into the classroom. We can have out our paper and pencil and be ready to learn and have our homework out.

4. Come in and get ready and start on time. Maybe the deputy could come to class from lunch. That might help us.

5. Listen and be quiet.

6. I wish I could get us less homework.

7. I wish we could come to class, sit down and get started on our work!

8. My wish for the whole class is to respect Mrs. Steward.

9. I wish people would stop being loud in Ms. Steward's class. It is loud sometimes.

10. We need to have more fun and more parties. And all As.

11. Get ready for class all together would be good. Some do and some don't.

12. People need to come to class to learn! They need to focus. I wish they would focus

13. To give me an A for no reason and to just be kind to people. Having a little bit of fun and not having all this homework. To be Friday everyday!

14. My wish is to get more field trips out of town, and to give us less homework. Homework Monday through Thursday, and Friday have no homework.

15. Class would be good if it started on time every time.

16. I want to show Ms. Steward my respect. I want to have an S (Satisfactory) for conduct.

17. My wish is to have us all on the same page from the bell.

18. I wish L and T wouldn't bring in so much of their drama into class so we could get going on time.

19. I wish I were the richest person in the world

20. Saying there is no homework! Saying we don't have to do nothing to pass!

21. I wish things would go in order the same way. So I know what to do.

May could certainly understand her students' craving for less pressure, especially since the school year was ending and due to the fact that many of her students qualified for free or reduced-priced lunch, they faced uncertainty during the summer months. What was most significant to May, however, was that a good two thirds of the class was looking for less drama and more stability in the classroom. May used this knowledge to fine-tune and reorder the interventions she had designed to implement as a part of her inquiry, and focused the next phase of her research on developing a consistent class routine.

Summative Data Analysis

While important insights are gleaned from the process of formative data analysis just described, as one nears the end of a cycle of inquiry, it's critical to engage in summative data analysis as well. Summative data analysis involves stepping back at the end of one inquiry cycle and taking a look at the entire data set as a whole, often in preparation for sharing one's work with others. New and different types of insights are gleaned during summative data analysis that cannot be gleaned from the independent looks at isolated portions of data done previously during formative data analysis.

While summative data analysis is one of the most rewarding and exciting components of engaging in inquiry, it can also appear to be the most difficult. The appearance of difficulty results from uncertainty about what the process entails, especially what to do with data that isn't quantifiable (i.e., student work, field notes, interviews, artifacts, and journal entries). Some teacher researchers even experience a sense of trepidation as they approach summative data analysis that can become paralyzing. If at this point in your inquiry you find yourself lamenting, "Okay, I've collected all of the *stuff*, but I have no clue of what to do with it now," you may be experiencing the first symptom of the common ailment "data analysis paralysis."

How to Avoid Data Analysis Paralysis

Data analysis paralysis actualizes itself by the avoidance of data. Data gather dust as an untouched pile on teacher researchers' desks as they continually forego looking at their data in favor of other tasks and duties. Thoughts of "I just don't have the time right now" creep into teacher researchers' head each time they glance at the looming pile of data on the desk. Eventually, they move the pile on their desk to the top of a filing cabinet or shelf, and there the data sits, untouched, for months, until so much time has elapsed between initial data collection and analysis that it just doesn't seem worth continuing.

Never completing summative data analysis robs you of the opportunity to learn a great deal about practice and improve the ways you and your students experience schooling! Data analysis paralysis can be cured and/or avoided altogether by confronting the data analysis task and taking control of the process by keeping it simple.

Confront the summative data analysis task. The first step to confronting the task at hand is to set aside a block of time in your calendar committed to data analysis. As you block out this data analysis time in your calendar, keep in mind that when in the summative data analysis phase of their research, many practitioner researchers find one or two longer blocks of time more productive than a series of shorter times.

As you cannot confront what you don't know or understand, the second step to confronting the data analysis task is to become comfortable with the meaning of data analysis for the teacher researcher and realize that while it might share some aspects of the data analysis processes used by traditional researchers, the purpose of data analysis for the teacher researcher is different. Lawrence Stenhouse, noted scholar in the practitioner research movement, uses the comparison of an agriculturalist and a gardener to provide insights into the difference between traditional and teacher research:

> In agriculture the equation of invested input against gross yield is all: it does not matter if individual plants fail to thrive or die so long as the cost of saving them is greater than the cost of losing them . . . This does not apply to the careful gardener whose labour is not costed, but a labour of love. He wants each of his plants to thrive, and he can treat each one individually. Indeed he can grow a hundred different plants in his garden and differentiate his treatment of each, pruning his roses, but not his sweet peas. (Rudduck & Hopkins, 1985, p. 26)

The traditional researcher is an agriculturalist, while a teacher researcher is a gardener. The gardener creates and tells his or her research story through engagement in summative data analysis. The process is nothing more than that—storying one's teaching practice, storying one's labor of love.

Take control by keeping it simple. Simply put, there are two types of data teacher researchers use to create their story of professional learning through engagement in inquiry—quantitative and qualitative.

Most teachers feel quite comfortable with the analysis of quantitative data, as it more closely aligns with images of traditional notions of research and they feel they know what to do with quantitative data. Data that take the form of numbers can be charted, tabled, and/or graphed to look for trends overtime and/or to provide comparisons and contrasts in data at a glance. For example, in implementing some action that May hoped would lead to a smoother start to her science lessons, May kept track of how long it took her students to settle into the day by writing the day's agenda in their notebook over time, and she graphed the results according:

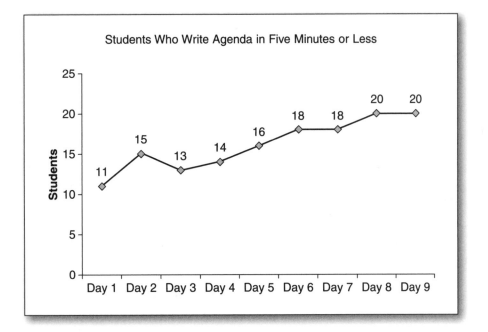

Just as was discussed in the previous chapters that it is important to play with your wondering and your inquiry plan as you are developing them, it is equally important to play with your data as well. Playing with your data helps you get beneath the surface and dig deep into your learning and the undercurrent of what is happening in your classroom. Playing with your quantitative data means more than just simply creating one chart, graph, or table and drawing conclusions based on what you see at first sight. Rather, it's important to look at the quantitative data in different ways. For example, you might average pre- and posttest scores and look at your class's growth as a whole. Next, you might use the same data set to look at individual students and chart how much each student has gained from pre- to posttest time, noting any outliers—students who made extremely large gains or no or little gain at all. What might be explanations for any outliers? What actions might you take with these students? Finally, you may sort these same data by students who made small, medium, and large gains to see if any interesting patterns emerge related to characteristics of students who have made different types of gains. Insights gleaned from different sorting of quantitative data can lead to additional ideas for sorting your data as well.

Teachers generally feel less comfortable analyzing qualitative data as these data take the form of words or images and don't lend themselves to the seemingly quick and easy construction of different charts, graphs, or tables. Ironically, while teachers feel less comfortable with qualitative data, qualitative data (particularly student work and observational notes) are often the most prevalent and telling type of data collected in teacher research, as it is naturalistic and helps capture the complexity of what is occurring in the classroom setting in a way that a sole look at number data cannot.

To analyze qualitative data, teacher researchers generally begin by simply reading through their entire data set once or twice to get a sense of what they have. They use the following questions to frame these first reads of the qualitative data set:

- Why did I inquire in the first place?
- What did I see as I inquired?
- What do I notice about my data?
- How would I describe these data to others?

With an initial sense of the data set established, next teacher researchers begin a process of condensing and extracting important components in the qualitative data set and categorizing and sorting these components in various groupings and configurations. Teacher researchers use the following questions to accomplish this task:

- What is most interesting about these data?
- What are some things in this data that stand out from the rest?
- How might different pieces of my data fit together?

This part of the process involves coding data, often accomplished by highlighting different themes or patterns in the data. This part of the process is similar to the ways May analyzed the 21 wishes her class shared in the example at the start of this chapter by grouping class responses into three different categories, highlighting each category.

To gain rich and deep understanding, this analysis of qualitative data requires the same sort of playful activity described for quantitative data—grouping and regrouping data in different ways and different configurations to gain new and different insights. The most critical and useful insights for practice are then drawn from the many sorts and re-sorts of data, and these insights form the basis for the teacher researcher to "story" her learning. As the teacher researcher stories her learning, she uses excerpts from the data to support her critical insights or claims about her work, and reflects on the following questions:

- What have I learned about myself as a teacher?
- What have I learned about my students?
- What have I learned about the larger context of schools and schooling?
- What are the implications of what I have learned for my practice?
- What changes might I make in my practice?
- What new wonderings do I have?

Chapter 4 of *The Reflective Educator's Guide to Classroom Research* titled Finding Your Findings: Data Analysis (Dana & Yendol-Hoppey, 2009) contains more detail on and examples of the summative data analysis process.

The Data Analysis Litmus Test

Unlike the litmus tests that appear in Chapters 2 and 3 to help you fine-tune your wondering and your plan for inquiry, the data analysis process is different for each teacher researcher, and therefore, there exists no one common set of questions that can be used by all teacher researchers to deepen the quality of their analyses. While it would be impossible to develop a litmus test activity to end this chapter like the ones in the previous chapters, you can deepen the quality of your analyses by engaging your colleagues in helping you scrutinize your data to be sure your summative data analysis is the best that it can be. In essence, you and your colleagues design a data analysis litmus test that is unique to you, your inquiry, and your data.

Teacher researchers who involve teaching colleagues in the process of data analysis have far richer inquiry experiences than do teachers who try to go it alone. Asking others to help you think about your data has many benefits. First, having colleagues help you in the data analysis process keeps moving you along. When you've scheduled a meeting to talk about your data, you must prepare for that meeting, and it becomes much harder to put off the data analysis task. Second, having colleagues help you in data analysis contributes to your ability to self-reflect and make sense of your data. You've already learned about the importance of talking with others as you defined and refined your wondering in Chapter 2. Similarly, as you continue on in the practitioner research journey, engaging in dialogue with other professionals as you analyze your data will help heighten your awareness of knowledge you've generated about teaching that you now take for granted, making what you know more visible to yourself and to others. Making your tacit knowledge more visible can often lead to significant discoveries when you are individually or collaboratively analyzing and interpreting your data.

In addition, talking about your data with other professionals may help you call into question assumptions or "givens" about teaching, a process that is critical to making your work problematic through the process of inquiry. According to Cochran-Smith and Lytle (1993), "The givens of schooling compose a long list, including reading groups, rostering, in-servicing, tracking, abilities, disabilities, mastery, retention, promotion, giftedness, disadvantage, special needs, departmentalization, 47-minute periods, coverage, standards, detention, teacher-proof materials, and homework" (p. 96). It is through talking with others about your data that you are enabled to examine and critique the "givens" in education such as those named previously. And it is through talking with others about your data that you are able to generate possible alternatives to practice as well as consider different interpretations that help every teacher gain perspective as his or her inquiry unfolds.

Finally, involving others in the process of data analysis can lend credibility to your study, as others are looking at your data and helping you scrutinize it. Your colleagues can both verify what you see in the data as well as push you to consider aspects of your data that you may not have discovered by analyzing your data alone.

To participate in a data analysis litmus test that is particular to your wondering, your research plan, and your data collection and analysis process, ask a group of your colleagues to participate with you in a 30-minute meeting designed in a similar fashion to meeting structure protocols advocated by School Reform Initiative, an alliance of educators committed to creating "transformational learning communities fiercely committed to educational equity and excellence" (www.schoolreforminitiative.org/). Prior to that meeting, organize and read through your entire data set once or twice to begin the data analysis process. Then, in preparation for your 30-minute meeting, complete the following sentences:

The issue/tension/dilemma/problem/interest that led me to my inquiry was _____

_____

_____

_____.

Therefore, the purpose of my inquiry was to _____

_____

_____.

My "wondering/wonderings were" _____

_____

_____."

I collected data by _____

_____.

So far, three discoveries I've made from reading through my data are

(1) _____

_____

_____;

(2) _____

_____

_____;

(3) _____

_____

_____.

Use these responses to your open-ended sentences to kick off your meeting with a brief, yet articulate overview of your inquiry journey to date.

Next, provide time for your colleagues to ask you both clarifying and probing questions about your work. A clarifying question has a factual answer that your colleagues may need to know to better understand your inquiry, such as "How long did you collect data?" or "How many students did you work with?" A probing question is open-ended, asking for you to clarify or expand your thinking about what you are learning from your data. It is important to note that probing questions are *not* suggestions. The question stems "Did you ever think that . . ." "Did you ever consider. . . " and "Would it be worthwhile for you to . . . " are clear indications that your colleague is *suggesting* interpretations of your data or action you take related to your data set rather than helping to *expand your thinking* about your data. An example of a *suggestion* disguised as probing question might be "Did you think it might be beneficial to look at just the struggling learners in your data and see how they experienced the teaching strategy you introduced as a part of your inquiry?" This suggestion disguised as a probing question would more appropriately be posed open-endedly as "What are some other ways you might organize your data?" or "What data do you have that don't seem to fit?" Ask your colleagues to hold off on *suggestions* until you've completed the clarifying and probing questioning process.

After questions are completed, ask your colleagues to discuss your data as if you weren't in the room. It is at this point that they might offer interpretations of your data or suggest additional actions you might take in the data analysis process to better understand your learning. Listen carefully to their discussion but do not speak. Instead, just take in your colleagues' conversation about your work. This gives you the opportunity to focus on reflection rather than needing to formulate responses to your colleagues' comments, and overall, it will lead to deeper insights about your work. Take notes on what you are learning from listening to the conversation.

End your "data analysis litmus test meeting" by summarizing the notes you took during the discussion and thanking your colleagues for helping you think about your data. Even though the discussion structure just described may feel awkward or artificial at first, if you follow the steps summarized at the end of this chapter with fidelity, you will experience powerful learning about your data that would not emerge during an unstructured meeting time. For more information on structuring data analysis discussions with colleagues and an example of how powerful such structured data analysis discussions can be, see Chapter 5 titled Helping PLC Members Analyze Data in *The Reflective Educator's Guide to Professional Development: Coaching Inquiry-Oriented Learning Communities* (Dana & Yendol-Hoppey, 2008).

Data Analysis Litmus Test Meeting

Suggested Group Size: 4 to 6

Suggested Time Frame: Approximately 30 Minutes

Step One: Researcher Shares His or Her Inquiry (4–5 Minutes)—The teacher researcher briefly shares the focus/purpose of his or her inquiry, what his or her wondering/wonderings were, how data were collected, and the initial sense that the teacher researcher has made of his or her data. Completing the following sentences prior to discussion may help the researcher organize his or her thoughts prior to sharing:

- The issue/dilemma/problem/interest that led me to my inquiry was . . .
- Therefore, the purpose of my inquiry was to . . .
- My wondering/wonderings were . . .
- I collected data by . . .
- So far, three discoveries I've made from reading through my data are . . .

Step Two: Meeting Participants Ask Clarifying Questions (3 Minutes)— Participants ask questions that have factual answers to clarify their understanding of the inquiry, such as "How long did you collect data?" and "How many students did you work with?"

Step Three: Meeting Participants Ask Probing Questions (7–10 Minutes)— The group then asks probing questions of the teacher researcher. These questions are worded so that they help the researcher clarify and expand his or her thinking about what he or she is learning from the data. During this 10-minute time frame, the teacher researcher may respond to the group's questions, **but there is no discussion by the group of the responses.** Every member of the group should pose at least one question of the researcher. Some examples of probing questions might include the following:

a. What are some additional ways you might organize your data?

b. What might be some powerful ways to present your data?

c. Do you have any data that doesn't seem to fit?

d. Based on your data, what are you learning about yourself as a teacher?

e. What is your data telling you about the students you teach?

f. What are the implications of your findings for the content you teach?

g. What have you learned about the larger context of schools and schooling?

h. What are the implications of what you have learned for your teaching?

i. What changes might you make in your practice?

j. What new wonderings do you have?

Step Four: Meeting Participants Discuss the Data Analysis (6 Minutes)— The meeting participants talk with one another about the data analysis presented, discussing such questions as "What did we hear?" "What didn't we hear that we think might be relevant?" "What assumptions seem to be operating?" "Does any data not seem to fit with the presenter's analysis?" and "What might be some additional ways to look at the presenter's data?" During this discussion, members of the group work to deepen the data analysis. **The teacher researcher doesn't speak during this discussion, but instead listens and takes notes.**

Step Five: Teacher Researcher Reflection (3–5 Minutes)—The teacher researcher reflects on what he or she heard and is now thinking, sharing with the meeting participants anything that particularly resonated for him or her during any part of the group's data analysis discussion. The presenter thanks the group for participating in his or her data analysis process.

(Adapted from *The Reflective Educator's Guide to Professional Development: Coaching Inquiry-Oriented Learning Communities,* Dana & Yendol-Hoppey, 2008, p. 124).

5

Presenting Your Research

Each year after I present my research at the Inquiry Showcase my district holds every May, I leave with a renewed sense of empowerment. I am empowered to do more with less and reach the unattainable. Showcasing our work not only provides teachers across our district with solutions to our own problems, but unifies a large group of educators who are committed to students and to maintaining a learning community of long-lasting professional relationships.

—Brooke Cobbin, Teacher Inquirer,
North Shore Elementary School

Presentation Defined

Sharing your work with others is an essential part of the inquiry process, and while this can be accomplished through writing and publishing your research, the most common way teacher researchers share their work is through oral presentation, defined simply as the provision of an overview of one's inquiry journey, beginning with the dilemma, tension, problem, or issue that led to the formation of the research wondering and ending with the presentation of findings, action, and future wonderings to explore. In sum, the oral presentation is the research story that, like all stories, contains three elements:

1. A beginning (background that led to your wondering culminating with a statement of the wondering and the purpose of one's research)

2. A middle (a description of what one did to gain insights into the wondering including any actions taken in the classroom and how data were collected)

3. An end (statements of your professional learning that resulted from this inquiry supported by data and directions for the future).

The oral presentation of an inquiry is a special story of professional practice, steeped in rich data that helps professionals understand and communicate the complexity of their lived story as an educator. In *The Healing Power of Stories*, Daniel Taylor writes,

> We live in stories the way fish live in water, breathing them in and out, buoyed up by them, taking from them our sustenance, but rarely conscious of this element in which we live. (as cited in Haven, 2007, p. 14)

Engaging in inquiry and sharing these special stories of practice with others raises our consciousness about the critical and wonderfully complex work of the classroom teacher. And if we raise our consciousness about how much we know as teachers and professionals, we have the power to raise our voices in educational reform and change the ways schooling is experienced by children in positive ways. This is the ultimate purpose of the inquiry presentation.

How to Define Your Presentation

To define your presentation, follow these three simple steps.

Step 1. Create the Outline

Gather your inquiry brief, your data, and notes from your summative analysis. Use these documents to fill in the outline provided:

I. Introduction to Presentation

   A. My context (Include demographic and logistical information about who you are, where you teach, who you teach, and anything else of background importance.)

     _____

     _____

     _____

     _____

   B. What led to my inquiry (Name the issue, tension, dilemma, or problem that led to your inquiry. This can be constructed from the first part of your inquiry brief and may include references to literature you've read related to your inquiry topic.)

     _____

     _____

     _____

     _____

   C. Purpose statement (Write one clear, succinct sentence that flows logically from your articulation of the issue, tension, dilemma, or problem that led to your inquiry.)

     Therefore, the purpose of my inquiry was to _____

     _____

     _____

     _____

     _____

II. State Your Wondering(s)

     _____

     _____

     _____

     _____

III. Methods/Procedures (Frame this section of your presentation by beginning with "To gain insights into my wondering, I . . .")

    A. If applicable, describe any change/intervention/innovation/ procedures you introduced into your practice as a part of your inquiry.

_____

_____

_____

_____

    B. List the ways you collected data to understand your practice (i.e., field notes/anecdotal notes/running records, student work, and other documents, interviews, digital pictures, video, reflective journals, weblogs, surveys, quantitative measures of student achievement, feedback from colleagues, and literature).

_____

_____

_____

_____

    C. Describe how you analyzed your data.

_____

_____

_____

_____

IV. State Your Learning and Support It With Data.

These succinct, one-sentence statements summarize the most critical and useful insights for practice that you drew from the many sorts and re-sorts of data throughout the summative data analysis process. These statements are constructed to "story" your learning. Think about the most logical ways to order your statements of learning and record them below. (Frame this section of your presentation by beginning with "As a result of analyzing my data, two/three/four[1] important things I learned include . . .")

---

[1]There is no magic number of learning statements that a teacher researcher constructs about learning. The number of learning statements will be dependent on your inquiry and data analysis process.

A. Learning Statement 1

_____

_____

_____

_____

B. Learning Statement 2

_____

_____

_____

_____

C. Learning Statement 3

_____

_____

_____

_____

V. Concluding Thoughts

A. General reflection on the specific inquiry completed (i.e., what you learned because of engaging in this work about yourself, your teaching, your subject matter, your students, schools and schooling, policy, etc.)

_____

_____

_____

_____

_____

_____

_____

_____

B. Directions for the future (i.e., changes you will make or have made to practice, new wonderings you now have as a result of this work)

_____

_____

_____

_____

_____

_____

_____

Step 2. Construct Powerpoint Slides

Now that you've outlined your presentation, look back at your outline piece by piece and consider visuals that will help the audience follow your presentation as the story of your research unfolds. Visuals can take the form of text (such as the statement of your wondering or bulleted points that highlight key aspects of what you plan to say). Visuals can also take the form of images related to the points you are making during each component of your presentation (i.e., real pictures, clip art, screen captures, tables, graphs, charts, and/or scanned documents, such as student work). Finally, visuals can be a combination of both text and image.

The creation of PowerPoint slides is a great way to add a visual component to your presentation and can be very effectively used as an aid to help you communicate the essence of your inquiry experience. A number of wonderful websites exist that can help you think about the essentials of an effective PowerPoint presentation. The most important thing to remember about creating an effective PowerPoint presentation is to keep it simple! Remember, the PowerPoint is not the presenter—you are! The PowerPoint slides serve as a tool to enhance or emphasize points you wish to make about your inquiry, not to tell your entire inquiry story. Some of the most important aspects of keeping your PowerPoint simple appear next.

**Effective Powerpoint
Presentations—Keep it Simple!**

Limit

- Information to the essentials
- Number of slides
- Special effects
- Fancy fonts

Use

- Key phrases
- Large font sizes (between 18 and 48 point is the general range)
- Colors that contrast
- Clip art and graphics to balance the slide—not overwhelm it

Keeping these important aspects in mind, pause now to create a series of PowerPoint slides to follow the outline of your presentation created in step one. These slides might include the following:

- One slide: Title slide (Includes the title of your presentation, your name, your position, and contact information)
- One slide: Background (what led to your inquiry question)
- One slide: Statement of your wondering
- Two or three slides: What you did and how you collected data
- Five to ten slides: What you learned (supported by data)
- One slide: Next steps—Where you are headed in the future

Step 3: Practice

With your slides now constructed, it's a good idea to run through the slides from beginning to end to get a sense of how your presentation will flow as a whole. Running through your slides will no doubt lead to some edits and tweaks to what you initially constructed. This, in turn, will leave you with a solid foundation for your inquiry presentation.

While you have now created an outline and accompanying PowerPoint slides for your presentation, it's important to realize that rarely does an outstanding presentation result from one practice session, one look at the slides you created as a whole. Just like the development of your wondering, your inquiry plan, and your data analysis, it takes time, tweaking, and actually playing with changes and adjustments to your presentation to get it just right. Hence, it's important to take some time to play with your presentation. The purpose of the final section of this chapter is to help you do so by taking the inquiry presentation litmus test.

The Presentation Litmus Test

Chemists use a litmus test to determine if a substance is an acid or a base. You will use a litmus test to determine if the presentation you created to share your inquiry with others is the best it can be to help others learn from your research. Similar to the wondering and inquiry brief litmus tests, the inquiry presentation litmus test consists of a series of questions that will help you refine your presentation.

Begin by printing your PowerPoint presentation. You can take notes on and edit this printout as you progress through the litmus test.

Question 1: Does your presentation provide an overview of the ways you actualized each component of the action research process?

When doing a presentation of your inquiry, it is important to cover every aspects of the process, including the following:

- Background that contextualizes your inquiry (often incorporating reference to the literature as well as the felt difficulty that prompted your investigation)
- Statement of your purpose and wondering
- Description of your research methods and procedures
- Findings
- Action/implications for practice

If you faithfully completed the presentation outline that appears in this chapter, you will automatically have covered each aspect of the inquiry process noted previously. Yet to be sure you remember to cover the ways each component of the inquiry cycle was realized in your work during your actual presentation, pause now and check your PowerPoint slides. Be sure you have at least one PowerPoint slide that correlates with each of the named components of the action research cycle. PowerPoint slides not only serve as visual guides for the audience, but also can prompt you to remember to cover all of the important aspects of your research despite any nervousness you may feel and subsequent forget-fulness that might crop up in the heat of the presentation moment. Outstanding presenters use their PowerPoint slides not only as visuals for the audience, but also as cues for themselves to provide direction and flow and help them remember the presentation script.

Question 2: Have you provided enough detail about the context of your inquiry to enable your audience to ascertain the ways your inquiry work is transferable to their context?

One important aspect to remember about practitioner inquiry is that it is rarely undertaken to provide generalizability about practice. Rather, teacher research is typically about capturing the natural actions that occur in the busy, real world of the classroom. As discussed in Chapter 3, this is one of the reasons that teacher inquiry rarely takes the form of an experimental study with treatment and control groups. Recall that Chapter 3 illustrated this point with the work of Debbi Hubbell, who recast her initial experimental research plan to more closely align with her natural approach to teaching and in the process, better understand the relationship between the reading of fractured fairy tale plays and fluency development in seven of her struggling fourth-grade learners.

When delivering a presentation of her work and sharing her pro-gress monitoring data, there was clear evidence that her seven strug-gling learners improved their performance over time. This does not mean that *every* teacher in Debbi's audience ought to start using frac-tured fairy tale plays during reading instruction, as one might believe to be the case if the purpose of teacher research was to be generaliz-able. Debbi selected a fluency progress monitoring tool as one form of data to capture action in *her* classroom, not as a proven, valid, and reliable measure of fluency development so that her work can be gen-eralized to all reading teachers everywhere! Additionally, Debbi's sample size (seven learners) was small. Debbi did not select these seven learners because she wished to have an adequate sample size so her findings could be applied to other classroom teachers. Rather, Debbi selected these seven learners because they were struggling, and she cared deeply about finding some ways to help them become more capable readers. Finally, Debbi didn't consciously and deliberatively isolate what might be considered her treatment variable (the reading of fractured fairy-tale plays) from all other intervening variables that might play a role in her struggling students' fluency development (like Debbi's approach to the teaching of phonics and intonation).

Rather, Debbi integrated everything she knew about the teaching of reading in combination with her introduction of fractured fairy-tale plays to target these seven learners' success as readers. Debbi approached her research not as a scientist who wished to discover the best way to teach all children to read, but as a teacher who cared passionately for seven individuals in her classroom, with the hope of discovering some insights that might help her reach these seven struggling readers. Debbi's research, as is all teacher research, was designed to focus *inward* on informing her classroom teaching, rather than *outward* on proving a particular strategy will be effective for others!

Keeping the notion of the inward verses outward significance of teacher research in mind, an important question emerges: "Is there any worth in one's individual action research for other teachers, members of one's presentation audience?" The answer to this question is a resounding *Yes*! The worth of Debbi's (or any individual's teacher's research) for one's presentation audience is in its transferability to their classroom. According to Jeffrey Barnes and his colleagues (2012), qualitative researchers define transferability as

> a process performed by readers of research. Readers note the specifics of the research situation and compare them to the specifics of an environment or situation with which they are familiar. If there are enough similarities between the two situations, readers may be able to infer that the results of the research would be the same or similar in their own situation. In other words, they "transfer" the results of a study to another context. To do this effectively, readers need to know as much as possible about the original research situation in order to determine whether it is similar to their own. Therefore, researchers must supply a highly detailed description of their research situation and methods. (para. 2)

Hence, for one's research to be transferable to members of their presentation audience and their contexts, it's important for teacher researchers to provide enough information about their contexts so audience members can ascertain the transferability between the presenter's context and their own.

Pause now to reflect on your presentation. Consider important logistical and demographic information that your audience needs to know to understand your work. Have you planned to describe your context in enough detail for your audience? If not, pause now and make some notes regarding additional contextual information you want to include and insert this information into one or more of your PowerPoint slides.

Question 3: Does your presentation focus as much or more on what you learned from your research as it does on new pedagogy or creative teaching acts you implemented as a part of your research?

Some of the greatest teachers are drawn to teaching by their creative minds that are constantly stimulated by the invention and reinvention of new ways to reach learners in meaningful and exciting ways. Many teachers thrive on creative pedagogy—designing and implementing new approaches to lessons and learning that ignite a passion for content and cultivate a deep, rich understanding of that content in their students. It is not surprising, then, that these teachers' inquiries often involve the design and implementation of a new teaching strategy or technique and carefully understanding the ways this strategy or technique plays out in their classroom. While they enjoy and benefit from the entire process, what excites teachers most about the inquiry is the implementation of the strategy itself. Hence, it is common for teacher inquirers to get stuck in that initial part of the presentation, where they emphasize and describe in enthusiastic detail, the "how" of a particular pedagogical approach that was a part of their inquiry work.

While this information is an essential part of the presentation and is often "eaten up" by the audience, it's important to not lose yourself in this part of the presentation with the ultimate result being the emphasis on pedagogy itself coming at the expense of *what was learned* about pedagogy.

Pause now to reflect on your presentation. Consider your description of any change/intervention/innovation/procedures you introduced into your practice as a part of your inquiry as well as all the data you collected and your statements of learning. Will there be balance in your presentation between what you did *and* what you learned as a result? If not, make some adjustments so you give due time in your presentation to both what you *did* and what you *learned* in this particular inquiry. Both are equally important!

Question 4: Did you support every statement of learning in your PowerPoint with excerpts from your data?

It is not enough to *say* that you learned something because of engaging in inquiry in your presentation. How does your audience know what you claim you learned is genuine and real? To help your audience appreciate the sincerity of and honesty in your report of learning, it is important to not only say what you learned but also to show your audience *how* you learned what you did through the sharing of data excerpts that correlate with each learning statement. The explanation of your learning statement should refer to your data, and you should include actual data within the explanation.

As we learned in Chapter 4, quantitative data are often presented in graphs/charts/tables. You may wish to present quantitative data in at least two kinds of graphs organized in different ways to help you explain different aspects of your learning. Similarly, qualitative data are often presented as excerpts of text from student work/interview quotes/open-ended survey questions and the like. You may wish to present qualitative data by including one or more samples of text that support your learning statement. For example, Student A's work might represent five students who made significant progress on an assignment after participating in a particular intervention. You can share this student's work and note that it represents the work of five others.

It is often quite powerful to show sample student work or quotes from students in their handwriting. For example, when explaining one learning statement, "My fourth graders were able to articulate the value of reading fractured fairy tale plays for their development as readers, becoming metacognitive about their own learning," Debbi Hubbell represented the following data excerpts on her PowerPoint slide in her students' own penmanship:

Academic Benefits ...

Dear Mrs. Hubble, I realy liked doing the fractured fairy tales. because they teach you a lesson. For example, the Cheta and the sloth play tought you to start slow and save your energy for latter, when you get to the finish line. I also like them because they help you read more fluently, and with expression.

Dear Mrs. Hubbell I really did like it and I would really want you to do more action fairy tales. And the last fairy tale we did I learned lots of new words that I didn't know. So it helped build my vocabulary. And it helps you become more of a fluent reader.

Similarly, in reporting the results of an inquiry that involved increasing access to his government, comparative politics, and economics advanced placement courses for students who ordinarily would not enroll in AP classes, teacher researcher Gary Boulware reported that "The majority of my students across all AP classes supported the implementation of a guaranteed C policy." Gary incorporated the following slides into his PowerPoint presentation.

In a similar fashion, I have also seen teacher researchers share excerpts from student interviews or discussions that were audio or video recorded to offer powerful evidence in support of their learning claims.

Pause now to reflect on your presentation. Consider your learning statements. Have you incorporated actual data into your presentation to support your statements of learning? If not, add some slides similar to those created by Debbi and Gary to support your learning with evidence and to create a convincing case for your research findings.

Question 5: Does the design of each individual PowerPoint slide detract or add value to your presentation? (Consider font size, amount of text, slide transitions, etc.)

The two most common mistakes I have witnessed when teacher inquirers prepare PowerPoint slides to accompany their presentations are having too much text on each individual slide in too small of a font to read and using too many technology "bells and whistles" in slide transitions or in building a slide that end up detracting from the presentation. In a witty blog titled "How To Change The World: The 10/20/30 Rule of Powerpoint," Guy Kawasaki (2012) asserts that no PowerPoint presentation should be more than 10 slides, last more than 20 minutes, and have any font size smaller than 30 point:

> The majority of the presentations that I see have text in a ten point font. As much text as possible is jammed into the slide, and then the presenter reads it. However, as soon as the audience figures out that you're reading the text, it reads ahead of you because it can read faster than you can speak. The result is that you and the audience are out of sync.
>
> The reason people use a small font is twofold: First, they don't know their material well enough; second, they think that more text is more convincing. Total bozosity. Force yourself to use no font smaller than 30 points. I guarantee it will make your presentations better because it requires you to find the most salient points and to know how to explain them well. If 30 points is too dogmatic, then I offer you an algorithm: find out the age of the oldest person in your audience and divide it by two. That's your optimal font size. (para. 6, 7).

Similarly, in *Giving Effective PowerPoint Presentations*, Scott Stratten (2012) echos Kawasaki's advice, with a particular focus on not falling into the "bells and whistles" trap:

> A common mistake is the overuse of PowerPoint animations and transitions during a slideshow. I'm sure you've seen what I'm talking about; the presenter that animates each sentence so it flies in, drops down, and explodes on the screen with an accompanying sound effect. What happens after that? Do you lose track of what the presenter is saying? Forget within three seconds what the point was because you were so focused on the effects that you missed the content?
>
> While the thought process behind these special effects is, "This highlights my point and emphasizes the importance," the outcome is often the opposite. People tend to get distracted by the effects. Especially with sounds, where the presenter can hear the whooshing noise, along with the few in the front of the room. The people in the middle think they heard something, but couldn't make it out and the people at the back are wondering why there is a fly somewhere in the

meeting room. Laptops were not meant to project sound to fill a room, so don't use them to do that.

Want to emphasize a main point? Put it on the screen by itself and let people read it. A good rule for effective PowerPoint presentations is to put up only your main points and use the screen as a reference. If you run through your PowerPoint presentation (which you must do many times) and you see a slide with more than five points, start a new slide. Your slide-show is not the presentation, it is an aid....

If only the main points are on the screen, the audience will realize their importance. Don't overwhelm your audience with techno-fluff. The power of technology is neither the point of your PowerPoint presentation, nor the strength of it. The technology should be used only sparingly or to reinforce the information you have to share. (para. 8–10, 13)

Keeping in mind this clever advice from Guy Kawasaki and Scott Stratten, pause now to reflect on your presentation. Look closely and carefully at each individual slide. Is there too much text on one slide? Is the font too small for your audience to see? Did you go overboard with fancy transitions between slides? If so, edit and adjust slides accordingly.

Question 6: Does the timing of your PowerPoint presentation fit within the parameters for the time you were allotted to share your work with others?

Whether you are presenting your work at a faculty meeting, a district event, a class session, a conference, or some other venue, you will have a designated time within which your presentation must fit, and it's important to remember that an ounce of PowerPoint slides often equates to a pound of presentation time!

There is nothing more unnerving as a presenter than having a session facilitator give a "one minute left" signal and you have only just barely scratched the surface of your presentation. This is such a common occurrence that frequently happens even to experienced presenters at such prominent venues as the American Educational Research Association that I wish I had a dime for every time I've seen presenters panic and race through their talk or skip large segments of a talk to jump to their conclusions without providing sufficient scaffolding for the audience to reach them. I'd have accrued a considerable amount of wealth from my dime collection over the years.

Occupying the presenter panic seat myself on various occasions, I've learned the value of timed practice. Today's stopwatch functions on iPads and cell phones make it easier than ever to complete a timed run-through of one's presentation. Ninety-nine percent of the time, as a result of run-throughs, presenters learn that what they planned to say in their heads takes longer to say in the actual act of presentation, and they find places they need to trim their talks to be sure they have adequate time to share the most important and poignant aspects of their inquiry stories with their audience.

Pause now and conduct a timed run-through of your presentation. Having a colleague or interested family member serve as a critical friend, listening to your presentation and providing you with feedback, is helpful in the adjustment-making process. How long did your presentation take? Are there places you need to trim and cut to the chase? What feedback does you critical friend have for you? Make notes of adjustments you wish to make to stay within the allotted time of your presentation and if needed, practice again and even again and again if necessary! After all, as the old saying goes, "Practice makes perfect."

6

On Your Way: Teacher Research as a Way of Being in the World

Inquiry has become my way of work. As a fulltime practitioner inquirer, I find my role as teacher is constantly stretching. I use inquiry to support, push, and question my work. Inquiry is how I collaborate with my colleagues; it's the language I use to introduce new teachers into the profession; it is how I teach my students. Inquiry has undoubtedly transformed teaching and learning for me.

—Rachel Wolkenhauer, Teacher
Inquirer and Teacher Educator,
University of Florida

Inquiry Stance Defined

This book began by making the case for the importance of teachers inquiring into their practice using the mnemonic 5 *E*s device to help teachers remember that studying their practice is empowering for several reasons. Studying your practice empowers you to

- *e*ngage learners,
- *e*nable other professionals to learn from you,
- *e*xpand the knowledge base for teaching,
- *e*xpress your individual identity as a teacher, and
- *e*mbrace all the rich complexity inherent in the act of teaching and learning.

Chapter 1 ended by introducing the concept "inquiry stance" as a professional positioning, owned by the teacher, where questioning, systematically studying, and subsequently working to change classroom practice, schools, and schooling to be better for *all* children becomes a natural, necessary, and never-ending part of a teacher's work. The promise was made to return to this concept in the final chapter and further define and unpack it, helping you to better understand, take, and live an inquiry stance in your professional life.

The term "inquiry as stance" was first coined by Marilyn Cochran-Smith and Susan Lytle. When these scholars first began writing about inquiry as stance in the late 1990s, they described it as follows:

> In everyday language, "stance" is used to describe body postures, particularly with regard to the position of the feet, as in sports or dance, and also to describe political positions, particularly their consistency (or lack thereof) over time. . . . In our work, we offer the term inquiry as stance to describe the positions teachers and others who work together in inquiry communities take toward knowledge and its relationships to practice. We use the metaphor of stance to suggest both orientational and positional ideas, to carry allusions to the physical placing of the body a well as to intellectual activities and perspectives over time. In this sense the metaphor is intended to capture the ways we stand, the ways we see, and the lenses we see through. Teaching is a complex activity that occurs within webs of social, historical, cultural, and political significance. Across the life span, an inquiry stance provides a kind of grounding within the changing cultures of school reform and competing political agendas. (Cochran-Smith & Lytle, 1999, 288–289)

Since then, Cochran-Smith and Lytle (2009) have authored an entire book titled *Inquiry as Stance*, carefully choosing these words for their title to suggest that inquiry is more than the sum of its parts (developing questions, collecting and analyzing data, making one's study public, and taking actions for change based on what was learned through the process). Rather, inquiry is "a worldview and a habit of mind—a way of knowing and being in the world of educational practice that carries across educational contexts and various points in one's professional career and that links individuals to larger groups, and social movements intended to challenge the inequities perpetuated by the educational status quo" (Cochran-Smith & Lytle, 2009, p. vii).

This is the essence of inquiry as stance. This is why one engages in the process described in this book in the first place. This is a way to live one's life as an educator to maximize impact, making life and learning conditions better for all the children we teach.

How to Define Your Stance

To begin to define your stance, keep three things in mind: (1) Inquiry is a cycle—resist the temptation to conceptualize it as a linear project with a beginning, middle and end point so that you feel "finished." (2) Reach out and connect to other teacher inquirers no matter how much effort it takes to do so, and (3) share the power of learning through inquiry with your students, creating rich opportunities to develop skills, knowledge, and dispositions that will serve them well throughout their entire lives.

Inquiry Is a Cycle

Chapter 5 helped you define and refine a presentation of your work. While making one's work public through sharing it with others is important; the danger of presenting your inquiry at a faculty meeting, district event, class session, conference, or some other venue is that after your presentation it feels as if you are "done"—your inquiry is complete. This feeling leads to the temptation to view teacher inquiry as a linear process, and focus on the outcome, the ending of one project, one exploration, one wondering . . . and then go back to the act of teaching. As a linear *project*, teacher inquiry is not a part of teaching; it is apart from it.

To cultivate an inquiry stance, teaching and inquiry must be seamlessly intertwined with one another, blurring the artificial distinction between teaching and inquiring. In geometric terms, it's important to remember that inquiry is best understood not as a line:

Develop a Wondering → Collect Data → Analyze Data → Take Action → Share

but as a circle:

As the circle has no beginning and no end, it has been symbolic of many things throughout the ages and can serve as a powerful reminder that teacher inquiry is not about the doing of an action research project that is completed at one point in time and is over. Rather, teacher inquiry is a continual cycle that all educators spiral through throughout their professional lifetimes—that professional positioning or stance, owned by the teacher, that necessitates the continuous and relentless raising of questions, systematic study of them, and subsequent improvement to practice. Although one's particular action research project might appear to culminate with the presentation of it, one's inquiry stance continues to be a powerful force and source of knowledge for self and others throughout the professional lifetime—just like the circle, it has no end.

Reach Out to Others

While tremendously rewarding, teaching and inquiring is hard work that can be arduous and even painful at times as teachers strive tirelessly to meet the learning needs of every child under conditions that are often not optimal for powerful learning to occur. Furthermore, teachers do their work within a society that often doesn't value or even understand it. Finally, even while great strides have been made in recent years to reduce the isolation inherent in the culture of teaching through the establishment of structures, such as professional learning communities, teaching remains a relatively lonely profession characterized by closed classroom doors and limited interaction among teaching professionals throughout the school day.

An important implication for teachers of the conditions within they work is that these conditions limit their ability to change a system that often doesn't function in the best interest of the children within it. A number of theorists have suggested that the isolation of teachers from one another and the hectic, harried pace of their daily work have been purposefully crafted to oppress teachers and "keep them in their place." For example, in his early writings about teacher research, Kincheloe (1991) compared teachers with peasants within a third-world culture with hierarchical power structures, scarce resources, and traditional values:

> Like their third world counterparts, teachers are preoccupied with daily survival—time for reflection and analysis seems remote and even quite fatuous given the crisis management atmosphere and the immediate attention survival necessitates. In such a climate those who would suggest that more time and resources be delegated to reflective and growth-inducing pursuits are viewed as impractical visionaries devoid of common sense. Thus, the status quo is perpetuated, the endless cycle of underdevelopment rolls on with its peasant culture of low morale and teachers as "reactors" to daily emergencies. (p. 12)

For this reason, living an inquiry stance means reaching out to other professionals, systematically and intentionally surrounding oneself with teaching professionals who share the same passion for reforming schools and the institution of schooling to make it better for *every* child. In the absence of situating oneself within an inquiry community, it becomes more and more difficult (and eventually impossible) to continue one's research. As a lone inquirer, some of your colleagues might even begin referring to you as an "impractical visionary." Hence, a critical component of stance involves seeking out and connecting yourself to other inquiring professionals within your school, your district, and even across the nation through such venues as the American Educational Research Association's Teacher Research Special Interest Group. Reaching out to others is an especially critical component of stance development for novice teachers to avoid being socialized into the profession by veterans who do not take an inquiry stance toward teaching.

Cochran-Smith and Lytle (1993) share that

> Communities of teacher researchers can play an essential role in school reform. Not only does their work add to the knowledge base on teaching, but their collective power as knowledge-generating communities also influences broader school policies regarding curriculum, assessment, school organization, and home-school linkages. Through teacher-research communities, teachers' voices play a more prominent part in the dialogue of school reform. (p. 103)

Share the Power of Inquiry With Students

The power of professional learning through inquiry is no accident. Inquiry is a powerful mechanism for professional learning as it is aligned with much of what we know about adult learning theory (see Brookfield, 1992; Knowles, 1990; Mezirow, 2000). First, teachers have *ownership* in and of their learning. No longer is their professional development something done *to* them *by* others. Rather they control and participate in their learning. Second, since professionals begin the process of inquiry by articulating a burning question that emerges from a felt difficulty or dilemma in practice, by definition and design, the process of inquiry enables teachers' learning to be *immediate* and *relevant* to their lives and work as educators. Third, engagement in inquiry is *differentiated*. Not all teachers are learning the exact same thing, in the exact same way, at the exact same time. Rather, inquiry establishes a path for learning to emerge for each educator based on his or her needs, prior knowledge and experiences, abilities, learning style, and current classroom and school context. Fourth, in large part, inquiry is *self-directed* as teachers take initiative and responsibility for the design and implementation of the inquiry cycle—selecting a question that is relevant and meaningful to explore, managing data collection to gain insights into the question, and assessing their learning through data analysis. Fifth, inquiry is *collaborative*. Teachers discuss and critically reflect on practice together through meaningful and structured dialogue, collectively constructing knowledge about practice. Finally, the process of inquiry is *active* and *engaging*. Rather than passively participating in a "sit and get" workshop, inquiry "turns traditional professional development on its head" (Check, 1997, p. 6), as teachers learn from their own investigations.

In sum, inquiry enables teachers to *own* their learning. In addition, inquiry makes that learning immediate, relevant, differentiated, self-directed, collaborative, active, and engaging. Because the construction of knowledge through the process of inquiry is so powerful, it makes sense to share the gift of inquiry with the students we teach (Dana et al., 2011).

By teaching our students through inquiry, we empower them to ask, not just answer, questions and to pose, not just solve, problems. This, in turn, helps us cultivate in our students the critical-thinking skills necessary to find success in the 21st century and to participate fully in our democracy. A number of wonderful resources exist to support teachers as they introduce inquiry into the classroom. Chapters 5 and 6 of *Inquiry: A Districtwide Approach to Staff and Student Learning* (Dana et al., 2011) titled Introducing Inquiry into the Classroom and Student Inquiry in Practice: The Stories of Elementary, Middle, and High School Teachers, respectively, can get you started in the process of introducing inquiry into your pedagogical practice as well as explicating the relationship between teacher inquiry and student inquiry.

Living the Life of an Inquirer

As you finish this book and a cycle of inquiry, you are well on your way to living the life of an inquirer. An important component of living this life is not just *doing* inquiry, but carefully and critically reflecting on the process and digging deeper into both teaching and inquiry each time you do it. Helping teachers dig deeper into teaching and inquiring into teaching is why this book was written in the first place.

To continue the practice of digging deeper, pause now to complete the following four open-ended statements and repeat this same exercise each time you approach the end of one spiral through the cycle of inquiry:

The biggest insight I gained about teaching and learning in this cycle of inquiry was _____

_____

_____

The biggest insight I gained into the process of teacher research in this cycle of inquiry was _____

_____

_____

Something about my teaching, my students, and/or schools and schooling that I want to explore deeper because of my learning in this inquiry cycle is _____

_____

_____

Something about inquiry itself that I want to explore deeper to become a better teacher researcher is _____

_____

_____

As you continue on your inquiry journey and incorporate the type of reflection you engaged in previously by completing those four open-ended statements, inquiry will become woven into the fabric of your professional being.

Through living the life of an inquirer, you leave an imprint not only on all of the children you teach and your teaching colleagues, but on the profession of teaching itself.

Mahatma Gandhi said, "Be the change you wish to see in the world."

Through inquiring and taking an inquiry stance toward your teaching practice, you become the change you wish to see in the profession of teaching.

Happy inquiring!

References

Adelman, C. (1993). Kurt Lewin and the origins of action research. *Educational Action Research, 1*(1), 7–24.

Ayers, W. (1989). *The good preschool teacher: Six teachers reflect on their lives.* New York, NY: Teachers College Press.

Barnes, J., Conrad, K., Demont-Henrich, C., Graziano, M., Kowalski, D., & Neufeld, J. (2012). *Generalizability and transferability.* Fort Collins: Colorado State University, Department of English. Retrieved from http://writing.colostate.edu/guides/page.cfm?pageid=1374

Boyd, T. A. (1961). *Prophet of progress: Selections from the speeches of Charles F. Kettering.* New York, NY: E. P. Dutton.

Brindley, R. & Crocco, C. (2010). *Empowering the voice of the teacher researcher: Achieving success through a culture of inquiry.* Lanham, MD: Rowman & Littlefield Publishing.

Brookfield, S. (1992). Developing criteria for formal theory building in adult education. *Adult Education Quarterly, 42*(2), 79–93.

Caro-Bruce, C., Flessner, R., Klehr, M., & Zeichner, K.M. (2007). *Creating equitable classrooms through action research.* Thousand Oaks, CA: Corwin.

Check. J. (1997). Teacher research as powerful professional development. *Harvard Education Letter, 13*(3), 6–8.

Cilliers, P. (1998). *Complexity and postmodernism: Understanding complex systems.* London, England: Routledge.

Cochran-Smith, M. (2003). The unforgiving complexity of teaching: Avoiding simplicity in the age of accountability. *Journal of Teacher Education 54*(1), 3–5.

Cochran-Smith, M., & Lytle, S. (1999). Relationships of knowledge and practice: Teacher learning in communities. In A. Iran-Nejad and C. D. Pearson (Eds.), *Review of Research in Education* (Vol. 24, pp. 251–307). Washington, DC: American Educational Research Association.

Cochran-Smith, M., & Lytle, S. L. (1993). *Inside/outside: Teacher research and knowledge.* New York, NY: Teachers College Press.

Cochran-Smith, M., & Lytle, S. L. (1999). Relationships of knowledge and practice: Teacher learning in communities. *Review of Research in Education, 24*, 249–305.

Cochran-Smith, M., & Lytle, S. L. (2009). *Inquiry as stance: Practitioner research for the next generation.* New York, NY: Teachers College Press.

Corey, S. M. (1953). *Action research to improve school practice*. New York, NY: Teachers College Press.

Dana, N. F., & Silva, D. Y. (2001). Student teachers as researchers: Developing an inquiry stance towards teaching. In J. Rainer & E. M. Guyton (Eds.), *Research on the effects of teacher education on teacher performance: Teacher education yearbook IX*, 91–104. New York, NY: Kendall-Hunt Press.

Dana, N. F., Silva, D. Y., & Snow-Gerono, J. (2002). Building a culture of inquiry in professional development schools. *Teacher Education and Practice, 15*(4), 71–89.

Dana, N. F., Thomas, C., & Boynton, S. (2011). *Inquiry: A districtwide approach to staff and student learning*. Thousand Oaks, CA: Corwin.

Dana, N. F., & Yendol-Hoppey, D. (2008). *The reflective educator's guide to professional development: Coaching inquiry-oriented learning communities*. Thousand Oaks, CA: Corwin.

Dana, N. F., & Yendol-Hoppey, D. (2009). *The reflective educator's guide to classroom research: Learning to teach and teaching to learn through practitioner inquiry* (2nd ed.). Thousand Oaks, CA: Corwin.

Delane, D., Dana, N. F., & Steward, M. (2010). *The story of May and her inquiry journey: Creating a positive behavior support system in a seventh grade science classroom*. Unpublished manuscript.

Desimone, L. M. (2009). Improving impact studies of teachers' professional development: Toward better conceptualizations and measures. *Educational Researcher, 38*, 181–199.

Dewey, J. (1933). *Democracy and education*. New York, NY: The Free Company.

Fullan, M. G. (1993). *Change forces: Probing the depth of educational reform*. New York, NY: Falmer Press.

Hubbard, R. S., & Power, B. M. (1999). *Living the questions: A guide for teacher researchers*. York, ME: Stenhouse.

Kane, K., & Darling-Hammond, L. (2012). Should student test scores be used to evaluate teachers? [Electronic version]. *The Wall Street Journal*. http://online.wsj.com/article/SB10001424052702304723304577366023832205042.html

Kawasaki, G. (2012). How to change the world: The 10/20/30 rule of PowerPoint. Retrieved from http://blog.guykawasaki.com/2005/12/the_102030_rule.html.

Kincheloe, J. (1991). *Teachers as researchers: Qualitative inquiry as a path to empowerment*. New York, NY: Falmer.

Knowles, M. (1990). *The adult learner: A neglected species*. Houston, TX: Gulf.

Lamott, A. (1994). *Bird by bird, some instructions on writing and life*. New York, NY: Anchor Books.

Meyers, E., & Rust, F. (Eds). (2003). *Taking action with teacher research*. Portsmouth, NH: Heinemann.

Mezirow, J. (2000). Learning to think like an adult: Core concepts of transformational theory. In J. Mezirow & Associates (Eds.), *Learning as transformation: Critical perspectives on a theory in progress* (pp. 3–33). San Francisco, CA: Jossey Bass.

Rudduck, J., & Hopkins, D. (Eds.). (1985). *Research as a basis for teaching: Readings from the work of Lawrence Stenhouse.* London, England: Heinemann.

Schlechty, P. C. (2011). *Engaging students: The next level of working on the work.* San Francisco, CA: Jossey-Bass.

Somekh, B., & Zeichner, K. (2009). Action research for educational reform: Remodeling action research theories and practices in local contexts. *Educational Action Research, 17,* 5–21.

Stratten, S. (2012). *Giving effective PowerPoint presentations.* Retrieved from http://sbinfocanada.about.com/cs/management/qt/powerptpres.html

Wolk, S. (2008). School as inquiry. *Kappan, 90*(2), 115–122.

Yendol-Hoppey, D., & Dana, N. F. (2010). *Powerful professional development: Building expertise within the four walls of your school.* Thousand Oaks, CA: Corwin.

Index

Accountability, 4–5
Administration, 13*f*
Adult learning theory, 84–85
Advanced Placement (AP) research:
   methodology, 41
   professional literature, 40
   purpose of, 39–40
   research plan development, 39–41
   research question, 40
   timeline development, 41
Art, 13*f*
Attewell, P., 40

Billig, S., 42
Boulware, Gary, 39–41
Boynton, S., 85
Brainstorming strategy:
   for data collection, 28–30
   for wondering, 11, 15, 17
Brindley, R., 15–16

CALLA, 45
Caro-Bruce, C., 15, 42
Christensen, Kathy, 42–44
*Classroom Instruction that Works with
   English Language Learners* (Hill and
   Flynn), 45
Cochran-Smith, M., 81
Collaboration:
   data analysis, 57–61
   inquiry stance, 83–84, 85
*College Outcomes Comparisons by AP and
   Non-AP High School Experiences*
   (Hargrove, Godin, and Dodd), 40
*Creating Equitable Classrooms Through
   Action Research* (Caro-Bruce,
   Flessner, Klehr and Zeichner), 15, 42
Crocco, C., 15–16

Dana, N. F., 16, 28, 57, 61, 85
Data analysis:
   analysis paralysis, 53–57
   assessment meeting, 59–62
   coding data, 57
   collaborative assessment, 57–61
   defined, 49–53
   formative data analysis, 50–53
   inquiry cycle, 2*f*
   process assessment, 57–61
   professional literature, 57, 61
   qualitative data, 56–57
   quantitative data, 55–56
   reflective questions, 56, 57
   science teacher example, 50–53
   summative data analysis, 50–53, 54
   timeline development, 54
Data collection. *See* Research plan
   development
Dodd, B., 40
Dougherty, C., 40

Earle, Sharon, 45–48
Elementary-school level, 12*f*
Embrace, 8–9, 80
Empowering the Voice of the Teacher
   (Brindley and Crocco), 15–16
Enable, 7, 80
Engage, 5–7, 80
English Language Learner (ELL)
   research:
   methodology, 46–47
   professional literature, 45
   purpose of, 45
   research plan development, 45–48
   research question, 45–46
   timeline development, 47–48
Expand, 7–8, 80

Expanding Opportunity in Higher Education (Gándara, Orfield, and Horn), 40
Experimental research design:
  case example, 35–36
  research plan development, 34–36
Express, 8, 80

5 *Es* mnemonic device:
  embrace, 8–9, 80
  enable, 7, 80
  engage, 5–7, 80
  expand, 7–8, 80
  express, 8, 80
  for teacher research, 5–9, 79–80
  illustration, 5*f*
Flessner, R., 15, 42
Flynn, K. M., 45
Foreign Language, 13*f*
Formative data analysis, 50–53

Gándara, P. C., 40
Giving Effective PowerPoint Presentations (Stratten), 76–77
Godin, D., 40
Grade-level examples, 12–13*f*

Hargrove, L., 40
Healing Power of Stories, The (Taylor), 64
High Quality Instruction That Transforms (Wisconsin Department of Public Instruction), 42
High-stakes testing, 4–5, 6
Hill, J. D., 45
Horn, C. L., 40
"How To Change The World: The 10/20/30 Rule of PowerPoint" (Kawasaki), 76

"I Know an Old Lady" 31
Inquiry as Stance (Cochran-Smith and Lytle), 81
Inquiry cycle, 2*f*, 81–83
Inquiry (Dana, Thomas, and Boynton), 85
Inquiry overboard syndrome, 36–37
Inquiry stance:
  adult learning theory, 84–85
  collaborative inquiry, 83–84, 85
  defined, 9, 79–81
  defining your stance, 81–85
  5 *Es* mnemonic device for, 79–80
  inquiry cycle, 81–83
  professional literature, 81, 85
  reflective statements, 85–86
  self-directed learning, 84–85

Internet resources, 59
Interwrite pad, 21–22

Jian, S., 40

Kawasaki, G., 76
Klehr, M., 15, 42
Klopfenstein, K., 40

Language arts, 12*f*
Legislation, 4–5, 45
Link Between Advanced Placement Experience and Early College Success (Klopfenstein, and Thomas), 40
Lytle, S., 81

Math, 12*f*
Mellor, L., 40
Meyers, E., 15
Music, 13*f*

National Association for the Education of Young Children (NAEYC), 16
National Council for Teachers of English (NCTE), 16
National Council for Teachers of Mathematics (NCTM), 16
National Council for the Social Studies (NCSS), 16
National Educational Longitudinal Study of 1988, 42
National Science Standards, 50
National Science Teachers Association (NSTA), 16, 50
No Child Left Behind Act (NCLB), 4–5, 45

Orfield, G., 40

Phi Delta Kappan, 42
Physical Education, 13*f*
PowerPoint presentation:
  guidelines for, 69, 75–77
  inquiry process alignment, 70–71
  slides preparation, 68–69
  special effects, 76–77
  10/20/30 rule, 76
Professional journals, 16, 42
Professional literature:
  Advanced Placement (AP) research, 40
  data analysis, 57, 61
  English Language Learner (ELL) research, 45
  for wondering, 15–16
  inquiry stance, 81, 85

research plan development, 28, 33–34
research presentation, 64, 76–77
service learning research, 42–43
Professional organizations, 16, 50–51

Raising the Bar (Attewell and
    Domina), 40
Reading strategy, 11, 15–16
*Reflective Educator's Guide to Classroom
    Research, The* (Dana and Yendol-
    Hoppey), 16, 28, 57, 61
*Relationship Between Advanced Placement
    and College Graduation, The*
    (Dougherty, Mellor, and Jian), 40
Research plan development:
    Advanced Placement (AP) research,
        39–41
    brainstorming strategy, 28–30
    case examples, 35–36, 39–48
    Data Collection Brainstorm Chart, 29f
    data collection process, 27–28
    data collection strategies, 28–30
    data collection techniques, 28
    defined, 27–28
    defining your plan, 28–30
    English Language Learner (ELL)
        research, 45–48
    experimental research design, 34–36
    inquiry cycle, 2f
    inquiry overboard syndrome, 36–37
    inquiry plan feasibility, 36–38
    inquiry plan flexibility, 38–39
    multiple data sources, 32–33
    process assessment, 30–39
    professional literature, 28, 33–34
    service learning research, 42–44
    strategy alignment, 31–32
    working the dialectic, 37–38
Research presentation:
    creative pedagogy focus, 73
    defined, 63–64
    defining your presentation, 64–70
    inquiry cycle, 2f
    inquiry process alignment, 70–71
    instructional transferability, 71–72
    learning statements, 73–75
    outline guidelines, 64–68
    PowerPoint guidelines, 69, 75–77
    PowerPoint slides, 68–69, 70–71,
        75–77
    practice session, 69–70, 78
    presentation format, 64
    process assessment, 70–78
    professional literature, 64, 76–77

technological special effects, 76–77
    time allotment, 77–78
Rust, F., 15

School Reform Initiative, 59
Science, 12f
Secondary-school level, 12–13f
Service learning research:
    methodology, 43–44
    professional literature, 42–43
    purpose of, 42–44
    research plan development, 42–44
    research question, 43
    timeline development, 44
Sheltered Instruction Observation
    Protocol, 45
Social Studies, 12f, 13f
Stratten, S., 76–77
Subject-area examples, 12–13f
Summative data analysis, 50–53, 54

Taking Action With Teacher Research
    (Meyers and Rust), 15
Talking strategy, 11, 14–15
Taylor, D., 64
Teacher research:
    defined, 1–2
    defining your research, 3–4
    5 *Es* mnemonic device for, 5–9, 79–80
    inquiry cycle, 2f
    legislative impact, 4–5
    multiple models of, 1–2
    on curriculum, 3
    on individual learners, 3
    on instructional strategies, 3–4
    practitioners as researcher, 1
    See also Inquiry stance
Technology Education, 13f
Thomas, C., 85
Thomas, M. K., 40
Thurston, D., 40
Timeline development:
    Advanced Placement (AP) research, 41
    data analysis, 54
    English Language Learner (ELL)
        research, 47–48
    research presentation, 77–78
    service learning research, 44

Wisconsin Department of Public
    Instruction, 42
Wondering:
    brainstorming strategy, 11, 15, 17
    defined, 10–11

defining your wondering, 11–16
dichotomous questions, 24–25
grade-level examples, 12–13*f*
inquiry cycle, 2*f*
meaningful inquiry, 21–22
passionate inquiry, 17–19
process assessment, 17–26
professional literature, 15–16
professional organizations, 16
reading strategy, 11, 15–16
specific inquiry, 26

student-learning focus, 19–21
subject-area examples, 12–13*f*
talking strategy, 11, 14–15
teacher-practice focus, 22–24
teaching-practice examples, 13–14*f*
Working the dialectic, 37–38

Yendol-Hoppey, D., 16, 28,
   57, 61

Zeichner, K. M., 15, 42

CORWIN
A SAGE Company

The Corwin logo—a raven striding across an open book—represents the union of courage and learning. Corwin is committed to improving education for all learners by publishing books and other professional development resources for those serving the field of PreK–12 education. By providing practical, hands-on materials, Corwin continues to carry out the promise of its motto: **"Helping Educators Do Their Work Better."**